I0786398

Books by Alan Pakaln
(In print, on Amazon.com and bookstores, also in ebook and Kindle)

The Feast of San Gennaro, Little Italy, New York, 1971:
A Photographic Essay, The People, Food, Activities
© 2017
(All photographs included in *New York Shadow: Behind The Scenes*
and, *NYC: B&W: Photographs, 1965-2018*)

La Festa di San Gennaro
© 2017
(Italian translation: *The Feast of San Gennaro, Little Italy, New York, 1971*)

New York Shadow: Behind The Scenes
© 2018
Coney Island, 1965
Night from a Car Window, 1965
The Feast of San Gennaro, Little Italy, 1971
Manhattan, Washington Heights, c. 1972
Bellevue Hospital, 1982
Times Square from a Bus, 2000
NYC Outtakes, 1970 – 2009
West Side, Lower Manhattan, 2018

NYC: B&W: Photographs, 1965-2018
© 2019
(Black and white photographs, uncoated paper,
first published as *New York Shadow: Behind The Scenes*)

Robot Desires: The Social Behavior of Technology
© 2000, © 2018

We Are The Machine: Only Following Orders
© 2019
(First published as *Robot Desires: The Social Behavior of Technology*)

Invention is the Mother of Necessity
© 2018
(First published as *Robot Desires: The Social Behavior of Technology*)

Into It

Interviews With Work

Into It

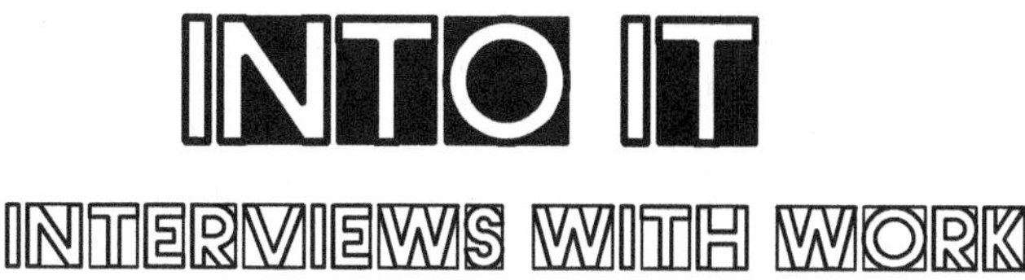

Film/Video Producer
Rehab Councilor for Homeless
Child Life Counselor
NYC Police Sergeant
Modern Ballet Dancer
Musician/Producer
Politician, Town Supervisor
Music Instrument Repair/Performer
Accountant/Olympic Athlete
Jeweler/Trucker
Flight Instructor
Human Rights Activist
Economist, Low Income Housing
ESL Teacher
Nature Photographer
Animal Social Worker

Acknowledgement

To all those represented here, for allowing me the privilege of listening to your stories.

Into It

Table of Contents

Year: 1994

Year: 2019

Into It

Introduction

These are transcriptions from recorded interviews that took place in 1994. At the time, a book of job-related interviews did not attract much attention, that is, besides Studs Terkel's *Working*.

I've always been curious about many things, among them, what people do to make a living. So I took my tape recorder – yes tape – and started with my friends (the police sergeant was one), and friends of friends (the documentary cinematographer), and did things like contact the US Olympic Committee asking for an athlete who did not win and had to go back to a real job (the accountant/Team Handball player). All of this on my spare time, over a period of a year.

Interviewing a range of different kinds of people was an amazing experience. For me, it was an excuse to meet someone very interesting and to ask questions about their lives - how often do you get the chance to do that?

Transcribing spoken words from recordings at that time was arduous – no speech recognition software – just a foot pedal on a tape playback machine. These transcript are only edited to remove some ums, and ohs, and my questions and comments. It does seem as though they are telling a story – and they are – but actually it was a conversation.

It's life stories: experiences told from a subjective viewpoint, bringing the human experience to where we can see it - each story spoken in the language of the inventor.

Into It

Merav
Film/Video Producer

I first went to photography school and I studied for two years from 8 o'clock in the morning to 6 o'clock in the evening, photography, chemistry, optics, and projects that they gave us. When I left the school, I started to work as an assistant for a fashion

photographer. Then I decided I'm not the type to work for other people. I just have this bug, so I left him and I decided I'm going to go on my own. The designer somehow learned my name and called me and I started to shoot for him and I made enough money. I also worked as a photographer for a big photography studio for a while. It was very boring. My photography teacher came to visit in New York, and she told me about this place. I kept in touch with people in the field. You can hear about jobs from people in the field you want to be in. You have to be a curious person if you want to make it on your own or to do something different.

Since I wasn't doing the creative photography that I liked, I decided to take a break for two years, and had a fruit and vegetable stand in Harlem. I actually learned it from a guy who did it downtown. I saw him doing it outside the Bleecker Street Station. Every time I passed there, all the factory workers were jumping on this place, giving him dollars, dollars, dollars. I mean, the place was busy. That was 1979, and there was something exciting about this place so I stood in front of his place for like a week, every day. He was a big Puerto Rican guy. He had all Puerto Ricans working for him. But every day, I just stood and watched in the afternoon to see how is he doing it. So, then he saw me and I said, "Listen, I want to manage your store." So he was like, "Oh yea, really. You want to manage?!" I said, "Yea, I'll work for you. I want you to teach me everything." So, he thought, "Oh great, you know, maybe she wants to screw with me or whatever--woman!" He didn't object. It was too bizarre for him to object. But he liked it and he liked me, so he said, "You know what, Merav?" He used to call me Meraph. "If you're willing to work hard, I'll teach you everything." So I went with him every morning to the market, 6 o'clock in the morning with his big truck. I saw how he was buying. I learned about the skids; you can buy a whole skid of tomatoes, half of it is rotten, but you can buy it so cheaply. All you need to do is hire, in the market there, a few kids and in 2 hours they will separate and take only the good ones. The good ones were really good.

So, he taught me all of this, how to buy and how to market, and he taught me about the different ethnic areas of New York. I was only in New York for a year and a half and I was twenty four years old. Since most of our customers were factory employees, mostly Spanish, he bought a lot of Spanish food, plantenos and avocados. I learned a lot about Spanish food and after three months, I wanted to go on my own. Now, he came to me; he had to go to Puerto Rico for vacation, and he left me the store to run without him. So he left me his van and his truck and he came in the evening and he gave me his pistol, and said, "And take care of that." That danger never entered my mind. But after all, it's on the street. You go to the South Bronx, Hunts Point in the morning--the drug pushers, a lot of crime, a lot of robberies. But somehow I never thought about it; nothing ever happened to me either. But when he gave me the pistol, something made me very uncomfortable about it, that he had a pistol with him all along. He also expected some sexual things from me all along and I wasn't interested, so it was a very delicate situation. I decided that when he comes back I'm not going to stay there. And I didn't and I started on 86th and Broadway.

I went to the market alone; I bought avocados, bananas and some other items and started to sell--the same system, a dollar a bag. You get a real good buy, but you gotta buy a dollar a bag. And you fix it very attractively with the colors, the pears next to the tomatoes, next to the lemons. On the streets of New York, you can sell anything if it's wrapped nicely, and you fix it attractively. People will buy garbage if it's good. But if you give them a good buy and it's attractive, they're gonna come. And we started to get very busy and every time we got busy, the police would come and tell us to move. They wouldn't confiscate our stuff, but they'd tell us to move. Eventually I did get a permit but it was a hassle. We found out that across the street was a different precinct. So when they tell us to move, we just move across the street until the other cops come, and we had another two hours. It usually was on a Friday afternoon when we got real busy. For two hours, we got real busy and we make most of our money.

So I did that and I had an employee, a black man who was an artist, but a junky too. I didn't know he was a junky at the time. His name was Manchu, a very smart man. He worked for me and when we started with all the police hassle, he said, "Listen, why won't you come to Harlem? Nobody's going to bother us in Harlem." Harlem! He told me that there is a woman there for 8 years with a hot dog stand and when I heard that, I said that if she can do that for 8 years, I can go.

So, I went there and we started and indeed, I became very friendly with the hot dog lady at 125 Street and 8th Avenue, the heart of Harlem, diagonally across from the Apollo. And that's how it started and it grew and it became very successful. I got to know Harlem in a way that other people didn't. I socialized with the people there. I experienced all strife with them. I arranged picnics and stuff like that, so it was sort of an adventure combined with making money, and I made nice money at the time. But after a year and a half of, you know, hot, cold and in every weather you have to be out on the street, it's not that easy. Also, when I prove to myself that a certain system works, that I've conquered it, I get bored with it and I want to move on. I had two possibilities, to open a supermarket in Harlem, or to start something totally new, and I wanted to go to something creative. I also needed to make money.

Then I heard about video. In 1985, I had a car accident, a minor one but nonetheless, I had whiplash and I had massages twice a week and I got the idea that if people want to know how you give a massage, then there's a need for a video tape on how you give a massage. That's how the idea came to me, so I got more and more obsessed with the idea and I saw in my mind, the whole tape, how it should be. It's just like an exercise tape. So I went to a friend and I asked him for money to make this video. I told him I'll make him my partner but I want to make this video and sell it to people. At the time he was introduced to me by a friend, and he gave me fifteen thousand dollars to make the tape and it's been selling ever since. For a while, I distributed it myself; then I found a guy who's in the business of distribution and I sold him the rights to distribute it and he's giving me royalties every quarter.

When I started, I really did not know what video was all about. Somebody told me that a community TV center is giving a course for free, sponsored by the city on what video is, and how to use the camera. And if you take the course, you can also take their equipment for like a dollar a day and do something with it. So, it was ancient equipment, very old, but nonetheless, I didn't have to put down any money. It was all free and available and I went and checked it out and fell in love with the medium, and took their equipment and did some things. Then I bought a camcorder and just like that, started to do more. And in time, it led into bigger and bigger projects.

What I do is I put to film, low budget films, all kinds of messages from political to commercial. Right now I'm making a movie for an architect who builds huge sky scrapers and he needs a movie about his work to show his clients, because people don't read today. If you give them a video tape, a short movie about something, it has so much more impact.

When I run into a good story, I buy the rights to it and then I develop it. I write what they call a treatment and I develop it--who would be a good actor, who might be a good director? And I try to attach it to a personality and bring it together to produce a film. I have two projects right now. I realized when I started, which was in 1985, that a lot of things are going to be short, mainly when it comes to information. Compared to the amount of information that you can squeeze into 1 hour of a movie, it will take you about two or three days to read a book that will give you all that information. It might be a little more in depth, but as they say, a picture is worth a thousand words. This business of information on video is growing because it fills more needs. More and more people look to learn how to do things from video.

When I go to raise money for a project, I don't go and say "Look, give me fifteen thousand dollars and we're going to make twenty thousand." Obviously, you go to people who have money already, and you know, how many suits can you wear, and how many houses can you own? So they're looking to be involved, or that their name would be involved in something that is different, that is beneficial to society. So when I go to ask for money, I don't tell him, "Listen it's going to make some money." It's not really a business proposition. I enroll him in the dream. I tell him, "Look, people would be able to learn to give a massage." You know, you get him excited about a project. You don't tell him it's a business proposition.

I wanted to make gospel programs. I learned about this national competition of gospel choirs, and I called the guy and said, "Listen, I want to videotape it and distribute it." I love gospel music and I just wanted to do it. He agreed, because nobody ever videotaped the competition, so he was happy.

There was a teacher who organized it, and when he said this is O.K., I calculated how much it will cost to document something like this. You need four cameras, you need a unit, a big crew, and it took two days and two nights and a big auditorium. So you do a calculation; how much money it will cost you to put it on tape, to videotape it, and how much to edit it, and then to package it, and to make the boxes, etc. I figured that I needed about sixty-five thousand dollars, quite a jump from fifteen to sixty-five. I went to a guy who knew I was working in the field. I was already in the business for three years, so there's some sort of stability, not a whole lot, but some. And he knew I was hardworking and well-intentioned and he has a lot of money, so he didn't mind giving me a shot at sixty-five thousand dollars to do it and we made the program. We got four programs out of it and we've been selling them ever since, and they will always sell.

There isn't really a formula when it comes to film making, and how you structure a deal. It's basically a gut feeling of what I feel is fair. This is my formula, other people may use a different kind of formula. I've heard of cases where people paid 100 per cent; they don't take anything but I feel I have too many expenses and overhead so that I cannot afford to pay back 100 per cent right away, so I pay 70 per cent. And when the principal investment is covered and you have paid it back, then it goes to 50/50. There really are no standards in the business, but I just think what I do is fair.

There is money around; you just have to go ask people for it and it has to be for a good cause that turns them on. And if they don't get the money back, at least they either did something good or they gave somebody a break. They're around and even if you don't have direct contact with them, you can initiate it. If you work somewhere and you know that the owner of the company is a rich man, and you have a dream of doing something well-intentioned, like a good cause that will also pay back, there's no reason why you cannot go to that person with a solid proposition as long as you know your subject; you know what you want to talk about and indeed, there's something valuable there. There's no reason why that person will not listen to you.

You first send a letter to intrigue them and explain what it is you really want to talk to them about. I have a friend who wanted to produce a video about her brother-in-law who is a mountain climber and had a serious accident in the Swiss mountains, and a big rescue operation. He lost both his legs, but he still skis and he goes for the winter, to the Handicap Olympics and he wins all the time. She had a dream of making a movie about that and needed 80 thousand dollars to make that movie.

Somebody told her about the president of Cannon in New York, and she wrote him a letter. Apparently his son is handicapped and it immediately touched him so she got eighty thousand dollars in one check, to make this film. She made it and it was aired on PBS and it was very good. This guy has millions of dollars and he has a handicapped son so he wants a message like this to get out there. For him to give, and he gave it away, was O.K. because it was for a nonprofit group so it's tax deductible.

This is another technicality of the business. You hook up with a nonprofit organization that is your fiscal sponsor and then people make checks to that organization and it's tax deductible. Let's say I have a project like the one I'm working on now. It's called "Brother Ninja War On Drugs." It's about a guy who was a gang member. You know, the typical story--born in Harlem and got into martial arts and channeled all his energy and changed his philosophy and became a martial arts champion and went back into the community and started to teach martial arts to kids and get them off the streets in South Jamaica, Queens, one of the most drug infested neighborhoods in America with a lot of shooting and killing. So it's a unique story and I wrote a good proposal, two pages to explain what it's about, with a precise budget of how much money I need and I sent it to a few organizations that are not-for-profit and "need" oriented.

There are all kinds of community film centers, and film and video producers just hang out there and you can find out a lot of information, like what are the nonprofit organizations around here that could sponsor your project. Then they give you a letter and then you go to people and say, "Here, you make this check to this nonprofit organization." That organization keeps five per cent of the money you raise, but they give you the rest.

There are now tons of outlets, satellite and cable TV outlets that are looking for different programs that do not have to be within the restrictions of American broadcast TV, that could even be a little bit off. So these organizations realize that there is a need to help independent producers in raising money and making it possible for them to get money.

People will be more likely to give you money if it's tax deductible than if it's not and they really expect you to know what you are doing and to show them previous work. Actually, you don't have to show previous work but you do have to be very well prepared about your subject; how you're going to show it, what you're going to say about it. It's not easy; nothing is easy when you don't know anything about the field, but it's very possible for somebody to succeed who wants to be a film maker or make TV programs or documentaries, especially today with the availability of camcorders.

You take a camcorder, you go and you videotape a little bit of the subject you want to talk about. You find there are places around town that you can edit. You take your video and you edit and it costs as little as twenty dollars an hour and then you can make a five minute movie about your topic. And when you have a demo like this and it's good and there's a message there, and it's understandable, nobody is going to doubt that you could do it. It's very possible they're going to give you the money to really do it. You just have to be aggressive, and you've got to really believe in it so that what you're talking about is interesting: "There's a movie to be made," and put yourself on the line.

Now when you have a film, there are many companies you can sell it to. There are trade shows a few times a year in a few places around the world, not just America. If somebody doesn't know about these shows, and doesn't know how to find out about them, the first thing that he or she has to do is find more people that are interested in the same thing and interact with them, because information flows from people to people and he may find a nice group into film making. There are places with groups and organizations that have something to do with film or community media and somebody there will know--he has just been to New York and there is this and this trade show going on. You have to hang out with the people that are interested in the same thing and start working your contacts together. This is how I found out.

Due to agreements between government and cable in every city in America that has cable, the company provides the public free stations. So you can make your own programs and air them. You get a time slot and as long as you commit to a certain number of shows, you can have your own. Nobody can tell you no. And it doesn't cost you money to broadcast. You just have to bring them a program. I found two people that had shows like this and I offered to do them outside of the studio. I didn't make any money, but I got experience in putting things together and more contacts and then I told people I was doing weddings, and I did a few weddings and I worked for a few companies that did seminars. I offered to videotape for two or three hundred dollars and got more and more experience.

After I produced the massage tape, all of a sudden people were treating me like a producer. Once you do one, all of a sudden you're a producer. You directed something? All of a sudden you're a director. You don't have to be tremendously successful in your first thing. What is success? You have to get an idea, do it, complete it from beginning to end and have a product that you produced. And once you bring this to completion, the process is the same for other projects. So once people see that you really follow through, they treat you differently. They see that you're serious, you don't only talk ideas. I know people that talk ideas forever.

The terrifying part is that you never know if you are going to be able to raise money for a project; your livelihood is dependent on it. You can get so involved in a project and the dream of making it, and spend hours and days and weeks writing and Xeroxing and sending it to people. And it all costs money, and meanwhile you're not making money. And the biggest fear, what if you'll never be able to raise the money for it? But you know what? I know it sounds like a cliché, but if you persist, you eventually will get it. If you pursue enough people, you will eventually get the money. And once you get the first money for a project, when you go to other people and you tell them, "Look, this person already gave me $5,000 or $3,000 for this," and the other person will say, "Well, if somebody already did, maybe I could," so a second one, and a third one. You don't have to raise all $80,000 from one person. You can get $10,000 from here and $10,000 from this one, and that is tedious and it's scary but that's the way it comes.

You have to take risks. But the odds of winning are there too and when you win and you work on bigger projects, and then you eventually work on projects where you can pay yourself $50,000 for working on that project, and it takes three or four months to do it, that becomes very attractive. And then if you work on bigger projects and you have some percent of the project and if it sells worldwide, you can end up with a few hundred thousand dollars. But the road there is hard, and you have to be committed in order to do it. It's not going to happen if you give up after one year.

It's a serious commitment. But you can start in your free time, and you can do this anywhere, even in Iowa because in Iowa you don't have so many film makers competing. There are rich business people in Iowa. There are factories that you can go to, owners that have money. There are advertising companies in Iowa. And there are nonprofit organizations that will sponsor you if they believe that the project is important. And with FAX machines and phones you can do it from Oshkosh, Wisconsin and have a sponsor in New York that will be your nonprofit organization.

I'm not talking about "breaking into" media; I'm talking about just starting. In order to go to the major markets, you can still live in Iowa because you just come here to raise money. You may want to do a project in Iowa that has worldwide interest. But in order to do a job with Bill Moyers or whatever, you also need to come to meetings in New York. But I'm talking about starting, having a portfolio. Do something small wherever you are, like a five or six minute movie; half an hour with a Camcorder and editing that can be done anywhere today. Once you have a portfolio, then you can come to the big city, and try to get the bigger projects.

I don't think I have a good business mind. I think a lot of the proposals I've made could have been better. I just go with my gut feeling. I think I'm a fair person and I just sit and think, I want this, and X would want that. So I just sit down and think what would be fair? I put myself in that person's shoes. And when I find what would be fair, that's what I propose to them, and most times they accept it.

I basically sit down and think, what would be a fair situation? That's the bottom line, nothing too complicated. And if somebody comes and says, "Hey, that's not fair, I want more," I look into it and if I think it's ridiculous, I kiss the project good-bye. And that happens a lot. So, you don't do it. There are tons of ideas and good things that I can do and I don't have to change one thing. If it persists, it's got too many problems. Usually if things don't move smoothly from the beginning, I don't get more involved in them.

It's really six months to write a proposal, six months to start getting it out and another year to raise the money, but you can already start shooting at the beginning of the second year when some money starts to come in. To write a proposal about any documentary takes research. Let's say you hear a good story and it really intrigues you. Once you get into it, and especially if you want to make a documentary about it, there are millions of things around it that you must know and learn about whatever the subject is. Then you need another two months to write a proposal, because you write it and then you rewrite it, and one to two years for editing and making the final print. The guy who did "Boys In The Hood", he worked on it for five years before he finished it. And he made it, because he went to the same school as one of the guys who worked for the studios. It's again contacts, who do you know.

Most of the independents are individual people who just have a dream. They wake up in the morning, they have a dream, they want to make a movie about whatever and that's what they do. I always have a bigger and bigger project in mind that's going to be my next step. I almost feel that all my life I'm jumping from one thing to the other but when I look back, it's not really true. I really believe that consistency is the number one thing in whatever it is that you do. It takes a long time to succeed in whatever it is, whatever career. Even if you are a store owner, you still have to open the store and you have to invest in it. It will take you some time to get your money back and then, eventually, it's just money coming in. But everything that you do will take a commitment of years. So for me, after I invested ten years in this film making, to go and jump into a different career, I don't even dare think about it. Maybe it will happen because, you never know, but...

The simple man says everything is common sense. If you got it, you can have anything you want, anything that you can sit down and say, "What would be the logical way for this to come true?" And then you follow it step by step. And if you are greedy and you think you are going to make a million dollars from one project, it's not going to happen. You have to pay rent and you have to eat, but you have to realize that to live, you work for a reasonable amount of money. Don't scare off people and don't overwhelm yourself by thinking this is going to be the project that's going to make me a million. Not so. I know plenty of film producers that work on million dollar budgets and just made a good living while working on it. Then the next project, there's more money and more, and more, and that's the way it goes. Unless you win the lottery, or unless there's a fluke accident, and you can't rely on that. That's not the way mortals are.

I would ask someone just getting started, first of all, what's the subject that they want to do a film about? How are they going to go about it, and who are they going to show in that film? By the way that they tell me what they are going to show and how they are going to go about it, I'll be able to tell immediately, if that is going to fail. Did they put some thought into it and if not, did it come out of a lack of experience or did it come out of laziness? If it's lack of experience, that will be forgiven and I would see a potential there. I'd be one to take a kid like this under my wing and say, "Great. I'll help you do it." But if it's out of laziness, or if their motivation is to win the Oscar, or to make a movie to become a millionaire, then it's probably not going to interest me.

I would say that for any film that is just in the dream stage, the only advice to a young film maker, which sounds really trite is--put it to the test. Because if you would believe that it can happen, it will happen. Sometimes a project seems so overwhelming before you get into it. If you are not able to visualize every step of it, it's not going to happen. In order to keep the hope and the belief you have to concentrate, visualize the next step, and the overall picture. The number one thing is, you gotta believe in your project.

Into It

Byron
Rehab Councilor for Homeless

My father died when I was eight, my real father. My mother remarried and then divorced eventually after ten years, but my stepfather was like a father to me. They were both very giving. They helped out people so I guess I got it from them. They just taught me to respect people. That was the thing, to respect people no matter who they were. Judge not people by who they are or what they have, but how they treat you.

> *Standing on the Metro North train station platform at Marble Hill, technically in Manhattan but physically in the Bronx, I placed my hand near a trash bin, got stung by a bee, yelled, turned to the person standing next to me – Byron -- and mentioned I just got stung. Friendships can begin anywhere.*

My job title is Rehab Specialist. My job is to try and transition the homeless from the street back to so-called normal existence in society. So I get to do things such as teaching life skills, teaching them how to re-socialize. Probably the toughest part of the job is trying to get them to socialize with each other. A majority of them might just spend a lot of time alone with themselves doing the various, I don't want to say neurotic things, but pretty bizarre. Some people collect trash, some people collect newspapers. We try to occupy their time by other means, maybe by taking a walk, going to a movie.

Some of the clients that I work with were very successful doctors, lawyers, teachers. I have one lady on my case load who has a Master's Degree in Child Development. Most of them are schizophrenics. It's just something that kind of creeps up on people. The people who have the illness are fairly normal for a good part of their lives and slowly begin to deteriorate at a certain point. It's pretty sad actually.

I use what daily living skills I have, try to turn them on to them. One tool I use is just whenever they're having a hard time, I let them know, "You know, I have the same feelings. I go through the same thing, frustrations and so forth," and that kind of normalizes it and kind of helps them to look at the people that work with them as being normal. So if you met them, they can realize that you go through the same feelings, you have the same frustrations and angers and you get upset over some of the things that make them upset and you deal with it. It really helps letting them sort of reflect through you in a sense.

They're very vague lots of times, not willing to share a lot. You get blotches of histories and it's really interesting some of the places these people have gone to. One guy was a Colonel in the Air Force. Now he's living in a single room on medication. We're teaching him to take charge of his life. He's just about ready to move on, but it's just sad to think of...almost like a shell of a castaway man. We're kind of like revitalizing that, so these aren't throwaway people. There are some people on the streets that are there either through mental illness or misfortune. I don't think anyone chooses to live like that. I guess there's a small population out there that does but most don't. They just don't know any better.

Once in a while you really get to know one of the clients, but you never give them totally, everything about you. There is a degree of discretion that you have to use. It's constantly there. There's a fine line. For some of the people, it's almost like they become a close relative, you become that attached. But there is a minor degree of detachment that you keep. It's not like you would spend time with them on the weekends. With one or two of them I wouldn't mind, but it's prohibited. If you spend that much time with a person, they become dependent, and after a while they would become overly dependent and it's not good for them. You know, that's the whole thing, they're trying to break this whole feeling of dependency, trying to be more individualized.

This organization started off kind of like a welcome wagon back at the turn of the century, when all the immigrants were coming into the country. It wasn't as expanded as it is now. It started off as just helping immigrant families settle into communities and from there it just diversified into youth programs, seniors' programs. We own a couple of camps, but they're pretty much all community based organizations. The name of this organization is Goddard Riverside and the place that I work for is called "The Other Place." We work with "Project Reachout."

A typical day; usually the staff will take turns making breakfast with a client for about thirty people, usually eggs or oatmeal or something easy. We have people that are employed by us. They're paid a small stipend, anywhere from three to five dollars. They come in and make breakfast in the morning for the staff members, then the same for lunch, and usually we have a pretty big lunch. We get two of the clients; they come in and help and at the same time you're preparing these meals, you're kind of teaching them, you know, wash your hands, simple things that you and I would take for granted. The things that you do, they really don't know.

Then throughout the day there are different groups and activities. One of my groups is a "current events" group. We discuss what's going on in the world or the community, any kind of news. It's very interesting, you really get to see a different side of these people. I never realized how intelligent they really are. There are some that are interested in what is happening in the world and some that panic. They're afraid of disasters or anything that may seem catastrophic. Some of them really freak out if you start talking about crime, something that's going on in the streets, social issues that are pretty bad.

They come in, they're given temporary shelter. We're affiliated with about two or three shelters that are very small and structured, and supervised with like fifteen or twenty clients, tops. We also have two or three beds in a couple of shelters. From there, they pretty much stay with the program. They go to the shelter at night and they come to the day program which I work at and check in every morning. They are mentally evaluated and we have psychiatrists that come throughout the week and eventually if it's warranted, they're put on medication. From there, we try and stabilize them and eventually they get permanent housing. So it's not a bad deal for someone who's really been out on the streets for years.

They're becoming a part of our society again. There is a follow-up, informally, like when some of the workers become attached. It's the same in just about every organization that I've worked for, it's time consuming to do follow-up and the feeling is that they have so much to do within the scope of their own program that they can't really justify having someone going out and looking these people up to make sure they're ok. You know, sometimes I think it's better that we don't, because once in a while you'll hear about someone who sort of didn't make it. There's not much that you can do then. I mean, you can try and talk them back and take them through the cycle again, but usually by that time they've reached the burnout period and that's difficult to deal with.

The thing I get out of it is being around different people and just listening to them. A lot of the people are older and it's really interesting listening to some of their stories. You don't know whether half of them are true or not. I think I get as much as I give, I really do.

There was this little girl I became very attached to, one of my case load that kind of went above and beyond. She came from a large family. The parents weren't guarding the kid, and I think they had seven kids. There was one Christmas where there were no toys, no tree and it just really hit me in my heart. I was able to go out and round up a tree, donated toys and food. She became pregnant and I was going to go into the delivery room with her. She wasn't getting along with her parents at the time and she had asked me if I'd do it. I was out of town, unfortunately, or should I say fortunately... It's hard trying not to become too emotionally attached, but it happens.

An important thing is you learn to detach yourself. It's not that it's cold. It's just something that you need. You have your life, they have theirs and there's only so much that you can do in any given day. It took me a while to learn that. If you don't, you burn out. I think that was probably why I burned out in some of my earlier stages of employment. I just didn't know how to gage how much to give and how much to keep. It's been a long road and I think I still got some distance to go.

I think I sort of fell into it. When I was in college, I worked for a "Y" that had various programs. Back in the Jimmy Carter years they had the money, and the social programs, and I worked for a few of those. Working with tutoring, employment programs that pretty much allowed me to get out into the community and meet different people--rather political. Having to hobnob and go to different things, town meetings and stuff to try and drum up jobs and funds. So I think that's where I sort of got the bug to work with people, adolescents. I love kids. I'd rather work with kids than adults.

I got a job working at a private residential school. I became a teacher's assistant and a woman that I was assisting was really great and allowed me to do a lot of things, actually to teach some of the courses. So it was really a good experience and for a while, I thought I wanted to be a teacher. I dropped out of college and decided I'd work a couple of years. I have this thing that I know when I'm burnt, that it's time for me to move on. If I'm not getting anything, I'm not giving anything type of attitude. I find that I burn out on organizations when something just seems like it's a business and they don't care. I just can't do it. It's like you're a puppet or a performer. You know you're not there and going through the motions just to keep the money coming in. So right after that, I went to painting houses. I just needed a break. I didn't want to deal with any kind of formalized work. So I had a friend who had a painting business. That was interesting for awhile.

I had found a woman that I became involved with. She was going to school in Boston at the time. She had just finished school and was living in the Boston area and had actually grown up in the same area and we knew each other, one of those deals. So I decide, like well, this town's just getting too small and I decided to go up to Boston. Me and a buddy, went up without any jobs or anything. When we got there, I put out resumes, but I got a construction job working about forty hours a week laboring. Starting off at the lowest rung, below the lowest rung, digging ditches and hauling stuff. Then I ran a group home on weekends for emotionally disturbed adolescent boys. I'd go in at 9 o'clock on Friday night after I had worked a forty hour week and work until 11 o'clock Sunday night. I lived there with nine adolescents on the weekend and I just pretty much ran the daily chores and gave out allowances to go to movies, sort of like a house parent type deal. I did that for about seven months, a total of ninety hours a week between the two jobs.

I stuck with the construction and I did that for two or three years and worked my way up the ladder. Eventually I became an assistant supervisor. I did the inspections. The subcontractors had finished what they were supposed to do and I'd go in and inspect it. This guy had taken me under his wing, he'd taken a liking to me. He just really taught me a lot. He became ill and eventually passed away of cancer. I was kind of kicking around, going from job to job 'cause the construction industry was drying up. So I'd work a week, I'd be off two weeks. I'd work two weeks, I'd be off, and I just couldn't live like that.

I decided to go back to working at a regular job, more steady, a lot lower pay, but steady and something I could grow in. So I went back to working with kids as a teacher's assistant. I did that for about six months and the school year ended and I ended up getting a job as a case worker in a private school, pretty much like a social worker. I had a case load of about four or five kids. The kids that we dealt with were emotionally disturbed or learning disabled. A lot of them were court involved for dealing drugs or assaults or even murder for some of the kids. What we did there is we kind of stabilized them. We'd get them right out of either detention or before they were going to detention, kind of a last ditch deal for the kid. Like "Look, this is it, the end of the road. You screw up here and..." he was going to jail or a lockup somewhere. The school was pretty much set up like a regular school. What worked out for me here was my experience in social work areas and the humanities field which covered a wide range. I'd done quite a few things, and had a lot of experience under my belt.

There's a college in Massachusetts, Cambridge College. It's an adult college that I eventually went to and what they do is they put you through all this diagnostic stuff. It's a real effort to get into this place. They run you through the ringer. I mean at one point it was just like I was ready to-- "the heck with this, they're driving me crazy." You must write an autobiography and get ten or fifteen character references. I saw why they did it after I had done it. If you can get through their application process, the rest is cake.

So I got in there and I was like one of the youngest people. You had to have at least ten years of experience dealing in the humanities field and they can turn some of your experience into credits. So I had enough where I only had to take a few extra courses before I was interviewed for the Master's. That really opened the door up for me, just getting that degree. It's a two year course and I did it in a year and a half while I was working a full time job, going to school nights, weekends. I took a vacation week and did intensives where you can do a course in a week, eight hours, you just sit there. That year and a half fried me and I became very bitter, very hard to live with.

I wrote a seventy page thesis on mentoring alternative clients, pretty much like the kids that I had worked with that had been thrown out of the main stream. It's like using mentors to deal with these kids and train the mentors on how to handle them. It's a cheap way of solving that problem rather than sending them to training schools which are very costly. Most of the kids I see are just misguided. It should be something that would ease the pressure on the system. It's basically just taking kids and having them spend quality time with a professional. Hopefully, it would be somebody from their community.

I got married while living in Boston, but I actually lived with my wife for five years before. When I came back to New York, I threw a couple hundred resumes around, because I needed work and I got three positive responses within a couple weeks, which was really good. And that was with the Masters. Without that degree, they wouldn't have given me the time of day.

You just got to believe in yourself, got to believe in who you are and what you're doing. Life is a circle, a full circle and somehow you got to complete that circle, come to peace with yourself. A lot of people aren't honest with themselves, who they are and what they do. I know what it's like to have to go through all the bullshit to get what you want, but it's worth it. I don't feel any smarter. I did learn to use my mind in a different way, and expanded my thoughts, but I don't really think I'm a lot smarter. It's just a matter of going through the regimen of something and seeing it through to the end. That's the most important thing. Even if you think it sucks, not having any fun, and it's just this bullshit, just see things to the end. It's a problem with a lot of people who aren't successful, because they haven't learned to see things through. And I think that with the Master's, that it was really a pretty rigorous course and I did it. I busted my tail.

My friends are all driven by materialistic things, cars, clothes. I don't need a lot to make me content. I've learned to do without. I have my little toys. Everyone has things they're kind of spoiled by, but I don't need a lot and I think the energy that I don't use in trying to acquire material things is used in a more positive way.

I've always just wanted to be one to help if I can. If it's within my power, I'll do anything I can for anyone. My friends do ask me "Why do you work with crazy people? Why don't you get a better paying job?" And I just tell them, I'm happy with what I'm doing. And when I go to sleep at night, I sleep very well just knowing that I haven't screwed anyone over and no one's screwed me over and I made the world a little bit better for that one day, maybe not for society as a whole but at least for a few people.

When I was going through school, I was told to be a carpenter. "You're not college material, you should go to vocational training and they tried to push me into that. I knew in my mind that I'm a little brighter. Not that carpenters are dumb people, but I think I can aspire to something that I like. Now that I look back, I see a lot of my friends were steered. Very few minorities went to college. They either went off to work or to prison. I had a few friends that I honestly knew could have played professional sports. They weren't the brightest bulbs on the circuit, but they had skill, athletic skills.

They were just never really given the opportunity to fully express or excel into something. Fortunately, I was always a fighter. I was always the hardheaded kid. If you told me I couldn't do something, well, I did it. I don't know if that was out of spite or what, but if I was told that "You'll never be able to do that, you can't do that," then I'd do it, just to show people. And that's the way I've been my whole life.

Some day I would like to have my own program: small, very personal, and personalize the care that's given. My dream is to have a group home where I just have adolescents and the people that I hire would be committed. I'll tell everyone, "There's a little bit of money here, and we'll split it up. You'll get yours, I'll get mine and the most important thing is that the kids get their services and that you're committed to following through, seeing this kid progress and becoming a viable component in society." Most of the group homes are set up where the kids are bounced around and they're never really stabilized, and those are the kids that usually run into rips with the law. So giving them a little time now can save an awful lot of money later.

I'm a player. I live each day as it comes. There are many obstacles and I just work around them and I get over them somehow. Life is a game and if you want the good things in life, you've got to learn to play this game; you've got to be a part of it. You can't be on the outside looking in; you just won't make it. Go to school, get the education, get the knowledge and then you play the game by your terms. If not, society has a set of rules out there that are just going to shoot you down at every turn. They're calling the shots, you're not. If you really want something bad enough where you really want to do something about it, you can do it. You believe in yourself, and just don't let anyone else tell you differently.

Michelle
Child Life Counselor

I didn't see myself married this young--never in a million years. I wanted to be one of those professional career "Ms." women, and I got married at twenty three and that's really young. It's hard to accept, sometimes, what you have. I mean, it's hard to let go of those dreams sometimes. I have a wonderful life, I really do, but I guess that's what gets you through it. I grew up on Walt Disney movies, that whole happily ever after thing and nothing bad ever happens.

Michelle and I both worked at Bellevue Hospital Center. Located in Manhattan, Bellevue is one of eleven acute care hospitals that are part of New York City's health system. They say it is the largest public health care system in the United States.

My father dying was a big thing in my life. It was like, this just doesn't happen to <u>me</u>. That totally pulled the rug out from under me. That definitely led me into this profession. I don't know what he went through when he was dying. I want to be around that, like I want to know what he knew. I know that sounds gross, and like weird. No one was there to help me.

I was watching a show on 20/20, and they have a really interesting new program for children whose parents have died and it's kind of like a support group. Children come and they meet once a week and they just talk about what it's like when a parent died. I just think it's a great program, and one of the little girls was maybe ten years old and she said, "Well, the one thing that upsets me the most is that my father is not going to be there to walk me down the aisle." Like I always say that! And it was just so nice to hear that this eight year old girl felt the same thing that I do. I know what this little girl is feeling--their father is dying of cancer.

I work with infants to children, age seventeen. It's a whole department called Child Life Program. There is the Emergency Services and it includes a playroom, and one of us is always in the Pediatric Emergency Room. In there we work with the children and the families preparing them and staying with them during the procedures and kind of just answering questions. They have a child coming with stitches, and we'll tell them what it's like to get stitches. We'll do it on a doll with them and then we'll stay with them. During the procedure, when they're getting the needle, we'll count, we'll blow bubbles, we'll kind of do relaxation techniques. A child gets hit by a car walking to school, so they're brought into the Emergency Room without a parent, so we kind of take that role until the parent gets there. A lot of parents don't want to be in the room when the child is getting the procedure, so we'll stay in the room and explain to the parent, "You know, it's ok, it's hard for you to be in there."

There are rooms for children of 3 different populations. The first is during the day. If a parent or family member has a doctor's appointment, the child then waits in here while the person is at the doctor's appointment. So we're with the children whenever the mother has a GYN appointment here, and we form a really nice relationship with that child and then can discuss what it's like having a brother or sister.

Then the second population is if there's somebody in the hospital and the parent is going to visit that person and the child waits in here. In fact, I just did my thesis on working with children that have a brother or sister in the hospital, and you really get to know them well, and talk about what it's like having your mother in the hospital or your brother or sister.

A lot of times the person in the hospital is terminally ill and the mother will say, "Can you help me explain?" You know, the child's grandmother is going to be dying, "Can you help me explain to this child why all the grownups are crying?" And what's nice is that you get 4 or 5 different kids at one time, and we'll do an art project, but the real idea is to get them all talking, and I'll say, "So, Suzy's brother is in the hospital, what's it like?" And we'll kind of get a little impromptu--everything is kind of done on the spot.

The third population is, somebody's in the emergency room and the child stays here, 'cause the emergency room is just horrible. It's not a good place for a child to be. So the child waits here. We've had children come in and they just witnessed their father beat up their mother, and the mother was brought into the emergency room. We're the first person that sees that child. The children that come into the emergency room a lot of times are here from 9 o'clock in the morning until 8 o'clock at night when we close. They're here the whole day. We feed them and a lot of times it's the children's first time in any kind of place like this, in any kind of play or school setting so we'll see children that are 2 or 3 years old that aren't talking and we'll refer them to special schools, to therapeutic nurseries. So that also works as kind of like an on site screening program. The child's 1, 1/2 and they're not walking yet, and you want to know why.

It's a new profession. We have an organization now and there's a conference in Atlanta where papers are presented. You have to become certified, and it's all pretty new, maybe 25, 30 years old. When the adolescent mothers who are pregnant, come in for their prenatal appointments, they have a group for them and they talk about what it's going to be like. They get the mothers to talk to each other. And also, on Wednesday afternoons I work on a program, called a "Hallway Program." It's for newborn to children two years old. When they're here for their doctors' appointments we have a mat set up on the floor, and the Moms and the babies go on the floor and you play with them and work with them to get the Moms to talk about how we could help them. We can pick up a lot of things that might be wrong with the child and we can refer them, or we could help them.

Traditional Child Life is when a child comes into the hospital there's a playroom and a Child Life Specialist. It's pretty much required that any children's hospital have a Child Life Program now. Most hospitals may have just one Child Life person and that's it. Bellevue has 20 or 30 Child Life Specialists; it's very unique. We actually go into the operating room with the child and we stay with them until anesthesia is delivered, which is wonderful 'cause it's a pretty frightening experience going into an operating room. Before we go in, we discuss what it's going to be like. We go through getting an IV, getting the mask, and we stay with them and a lot of times the doctors will let us hold children on our laps while they deliver the anesthesia until the time he sleeps.

We have a sex abuse clinic which a lot of people are interested in now. We're one of the members of a team. There's a doctor and a nurse and a social worker and a Child Life Specialist. We try to work with the team in every department where there's doctors and nurses involved. The newest program is the Methadone Program. They just got a Child Life Specialist on the team working with the children of the patients that come everyday for methadone.

The whole profession is very developmentally focused. What you tell a ten year old is not what you tell a four year old. You have to know what they would understand, what they would take too literally. Younger kids tend to be very concrete. When you're explaining death, they don't understand that never coming back is <u>never</u> coming back. It's kind of just--they're going to sleep for a while. It's the older child who will start to think abstractly. I tend to be honest and say that I really don't understand it very much either. Also, I tend to use books a lot. There's lots of stories, almost for every experience like death, divorce.

There's a Child Life Specialist that works with the AIDS team and that's her biggest frustration. Here's a ten year old who knows that they're dying, that they have AIDS, and the mother doesn't want them to know. And you have to work with the mother. But if the mother doesn't want the child to know, then you really can't--it's the mother's wishes. She doesn't want the child to know, but the children know. We had a little girl down here and she's HIV positive; her sister is HIV positive. Her mother is HIV positive and her father is. The mother's been hospitalized numerous times, and she has not been hospitalized yet, but her mother does not want her to know. The mother just tells her that she has some kind of skin condition, 'cause her skin is really bad now, and she was down here and she was playing in the water table and her whole play is about death. She's throwing the animals in the water and they were burning to death, and it was acid, and then she talked a lot about the future. She said, "What is my future going to be like? What am I going to be like when I grow up?" She goes, "I don't even know if I'll be here." So, I always feel like the children know, but you really have to work with the parent, let the parent know that the child is seeing this. But this woman; it's been about two years now and she doesn't want the daughter to know. This mother can't deal with her own death, so she doesn't think she's going to be able to handle her daughter's.

I'll ask a child, "When do you cry? What makes you sad? Well, sometimes grownups get sad, just like you do," kind of take it along that route. We have lots of books about feelings and I'll pull out "When I'm Afraid, When I'm Sad" and we'll read it. We do a lot of art work, like "Draw me something that makes you sad," "What do you do that makes you feel better?" Just let the parents know that it's O.K. to let your child know that it's O.K. to be sad, and that you're going to cry. "Just like you feel sad, and then you feel happy, well, Mommy will feel sad and then she'll feel happy again." We stress that it's not you that's making Mommy sad. That's important.

I've never been hospitalized and I'm actually really bad with blood and stuff. My husband says "Why are you in this profession?" I get woozy. I still get scared when I'm near a needle or a blood transfusion and here I am helping kids. The first time I was in the Pediatric Emergency Room, I fainted when I saw the IV go in. They had to get me orange juice. And now, I'm wonderful with it, I just don't look at it. I had a sixteen year old girl come in with a gunshot wound where her whole leg was blown up and it was the most disgusting thing, and after a while I was looking at it. I guess I distance myself from it. I still have a hard time getting my own blood tested. Whenever I knew I was going into the operating room, I would have to have a big breakfast. There are a lot of people in this department that have trouble with the blood and I hear that from a lot of doctors when they're in medical school.

I actually wanted to be a writer, and go into journalism. But I always liked working with children and I never really wanted to teach. I did an internship in a preschool that I really liked. I liked the younger kids. Then I had to do an internship in the summer and again, I didn't want to work in a school or work in a camp. I wanted something different. I was very interested in looking into a Hospice kind of situation because right before I went to college, my father passed away from cancer and I think that's kind of what's driven me into this profession. When he died, it was like, this is more important. I was like seventeen, but I still felt like no one ever explained what was going on. There was never any social worker that came out and said to my mother, "Well, what about your children?"

I did an internship in my junior year of college in the summer and I absolutely loved it. This is what I wanted to do! There aren't many schools offering degrees in Child Life. I was getting a Bachelor's in Psychology at the time and I wanted to get into a Child Life Program, so senior year came and I had sent my résumé out, but I really didn't know too much about it. I didn't know there was any organization serving this profession.

I got a job at a therapeutic nursery, a school for children that are developmentally delayed, they have language problems. Walking through the department one day, I saw this flyer for a Master's in Early Childhood, Special Ed/Child Life. I met the woman and totally fell in love with her. She was really pro-Child Life. She said it's a great program, but you have to do an internship in Child Life and the school was real expensive. Classes are at night, and you have to do the internship for a year during the day, and I could just afford to do that. It was going to be a problem financially, and she said, "I know someone at Bellevue who's looking for a person. Why don't you take a shot, see if you can get the job at Bellevue in the Child Life Department and it will count towards your internship, even though you're getting paid." That's when I came here, and I got the job and now I'm graduating! I actually started the school and the job the same week.

I could never explain what I do or why I wanted to do it. Nobody knows about it. It's almost like a secret profession. I never read anything about it in my four years of psychology, maybe because it's so new. They're now making it a requirement for doctors here in medical school that want to be Pediatricians. Like in the summertime, we have medical students doing internships here where they work for us and they learn about children, about the program, so that when they're doctors, they can take it with them.

I really liked my college, but there was really not too much help, at least in the Psychology Department with finding a career. We had a career center, like how to get a job, making a résumé, but nothing on different jobs. I was one of those students that really didn't know. I mean I knew I wanted to work with kids, but if you work with children, you're either a teacher or a Social Worker, and that's what I was going to do. That isn't what I <u>wanted</u> to do. It's kind of tied closely to Social Work. A lot of the things that we do and Social Workers do are really the same. We do short term child care, screening, crisis intervention, education, recreation, parent counseling, child play therapy, preparation for medical procedures, support during medical procedures, assessments; it's a variety of things.

Now my friends are starting to make lots of money. I have a couple of friends that are lawyers and even my husband, I kind of get mad that he makes more money than me, and we're both the same age and we both went to college. But I got a little letter from this one girl that I went to a Cardiac Catheterization with. I was with her the whole day and when she left, I had missed her so she left me this note. I carry it with me for when I get down, when I think I could have been a lawyer, or I could be making a lot of money. I just look at that note. I guess it's that old cliché where it's like, "rewarding."

My husband works for a big company and he's in sales and whenever I have a bad day, he's like "Come on, I sell orange juice. Look at what you do!" I guess what he means is that this is something. It's weird. It's like when you go to a party and someone asks you--when I talk about my job, it's like the room is just quiet. Like, "Tell me more stories." But you forget about it when you're here everyday. You almost lose yourself sometimes. I find that most people do appreciate what I do. They almost put you in a sainthood, like "How do you deal with people dying?" You don't always think about how you feel when someone dies. Sometimes it doesn't hit me until a couple weeks later. It almost becomes just a job, and like Bellevue is just a place. Everybody asks, "Why do you stay at Bellevue? It's a horrible place." Well, it's just a hospital.

I've never cried on the job, but I would. I wouldn't feel bad about doing it. I think it would be O.K.. I have felt bad, and I've told the child I'm really sad about what's happened, a child who's been sexually abused, for example. "I feel really bad, I'm really sad for you." I've said things like that and meant it, so I wouldn't feel bad about crying. It's O.K. to cry. I think different people have different opinions on that. Some people might say that you have to be objective, but I've seen other people that I work with cry. I've gone home and cried. I've cried on the train.

Sometimes you just feel like you're just fed up, you're frustrated, nothing's getting done. You're trying to help these people out, and it's not getting done. You have a four year old child who's not talking, and you've told the mother and she doesn't see anything wrong with it. Then you've actually gotten an appointment for her to go for an evaluation, and she doesn't show up, and it goes on and on, and you know that child is going to just fall through the system and you could have done something. You see all the different abuse like the sexually abused, the burned infant, a teenage boy you'd hear was selling drugs. In a police chase he got hurt; now he's in the hospital and how do you feel? You have to be so objective; here he is, selling drugs. You're with a fifteen year old boy, you see a different side of him, but you know that you'd probably walk the other way if he was walking down the street. You run back to the playroom and make sure that your pocketbook was locked up a lot of times.

There are a lot of children, guys and girls in gangs, fifteen year old girls that were prostitutes, and you'd be so intimidated but then you'd talk to them and they'd be so child-like. The first thing the girls would want out of the playroom would be a doll. And the boys, you'd see them playing, or just coloring. "Can I have a coloring book?" Here's this sixteen year old leader of a gang who they found a gun on, involved in a gunshot wound and he wants a Ninja Turtle coloring book. They respond to you so well and they're wonderful, but you know they're going to be back on the street as soon as they get out of the hospital. But what could you do? You could do something; you've been with them for three days and they've responded so well, but there's nobody out there for them. You can't follow every single case. You never know what happens to them. Sometimes you do see them again. They come back, and that's the nicest part of the job, when somebody comes back a year later and they're doing so well. I mean, you never know. That's hard, not knowing.

I know that in some jobs you might feel like this is as far as you're going to go, but there's always something new to learn. How to talk to a parent who is upset. How to talk to a parent who is pissed off. How to tell a parent that their child should be in a special school, because they're not talking. A big plus for me is there are many people who work here that are really experienced, so I'm learning a lot. We get a lot of responsibility, make a lot of our own decisions, pretty much given free rein with what we want to do. It's pretty diverse. I'm doing something different everyday. That's a big positive--it's fulfilling. It's really been on-the-job training for me.

There's one man here who works with the adolescents. It just seems that for whatever reason, women tend to go more into child care professions. I guess it just goes back to the stereotypes. I guess men don't think too much about being a kindergarten teacher. They're teachers in fields like math or science. It might change now that it's being accepted, that men are allowed to take care of children. Even in my school, there were hardly any men in the classes of the Special Education Programs. There's not that much money in it either and for some reason, men are expected to make more money. It might happen to strike one man as interesting. Most of these kids don't have a male role model, so it would be great if more men got into this field. It's really needed.

I really do want to have children. But you know how this job has affected me? I'm scared to death. I'm so afraid that they're just not going to be born healthy. I've just seen too many babies born sick. That's a big thing, and also thinking that I'm not going to be able to handle it. As much as I'm giving these parents advice, it's like, "What do I do?" It's funny, 'cause my brother just had a baby and being with my niece I'm so different. The first time I held her I was so scared. I hold two week old babies all the time. People think you're going to be this wonderful mother, because you work with children. My husband thinks "Oh, you're just going to know how to do everything." What happens if I don't? What happens if my baby's eight months and she's not sitting up? I know that at five months babies should be sitting up. I'm almost going to be too paranoid. It almost makes you want to have them more too, because you see these wonderful interactions between the mother and child. Even though, in one case, the father's not around or the mother isn't around, they have the most wonderful, talented, intelligent, caring children. Well, how does that happen? That's scary too, 'cause it almost doesn't matter what kind of parent you're going to be. It's probably just a part of the child, and it's not all environmental. The kid's a survivor. They're living in this horrible situation and they're just wonderful.

The hardest thing with me, is that I was going to be graduating college and I didn't know what I want to do. It's really O.K. for students to be confused--you're not the only one confused. Talk to somebody, talk to your friends, they're confused too. Sometimes, you just find something if you talk to people, if you read and find out what's going on.

I went to a pretty competitive high school and I had an older brother who was kind of "getting out there." I always wanted to be a writer from the time I was little. I wanted to write a book, and I wanted to write a movie, and I wanted to write a song. I wanted to win an Oscar, an Emmy, and a Tony. I just wanted to have anything to do with writing. I gave up. Oh I still want to be a writer, but I kind of just said, "It's not going to happen." I just thought I could never do it. I won't do something if I think I'm going to fail, I just won't do it. You graduate college and you can get a job. It's like, where do you go when you want to be a writer? And I was good. I'm a good writer. I took all the writing classes. I applied to Syracuse, School of Broadcasting, and you had to do a fake videotape of you doing the news and I got in. I even got a little scholarship.

There is still part of me that is like--one day, I'm going to do this. I'm just finishing my thesis and I'm thinking of writing it up for a journal. But I get these great ideas and I just won't do it. I like the idea if I could be, not famous, but if I could have something that could live on, or like that would make my family proud, "Wow, look, this is her book!" Kind of that glory or that fame. I'd love to have it. What I do is so rewarding and satisfying but, wow, to be famous! I'm very insecure. I have no self-esteem. I want to go back to the high school reunion, be like, "Oh, she's the one who wrote that!" Just do something worthwhile. And I guess this is worthwhile. I just can't accept this. I finished my thesis, and I don't even know if I'm proud of it. It's probably really good.

Bernie
NYC Police Sergeant

I was already working in a fish market cutting fish. That was in Little Neck, Queens. I had that job since I was about fourteen or fifteen years old. I was sweeping floors first, then I graduated... smelly job, fish along with shoes, with caked-on scales. I cut there for a few years. I was working, hanging out almost every evening. I was painting quite a lot. That was probably the most predominant thing that I did in my life at that time--sketch and paint. At sixteen, which was the year before I went to Ireland for about a month, I spent a lot of time there sitting on a hill drawing.

Bernie is not his real name — at the time of this interview, "Bernie" was still actively employed by the NYC police department and not authorized to speak off the record. He is now happily retired. Irish Catholic, opposed to the death penalty, and, outside of practice, he told me he never fired his gun.

Then I went to college, part of the City University system. That was in Jamaica, Queens, across the street from Washington Park, which had the dubious distinction of being called Murder Park by the locals because of a couple of murders in there. I remember feeding the squirrels on the way to school and acting a little crazy to get through the neighborhood. There was always the possibility of getting mugged. It happened to quite a few of the students there, not me though. Acting nutty, having this wild stare in your eyes, to walk through the crowds, a defense mechanism at the time.

I majored in art. I did very well in the art class, drawing workshops, sculpture and all that other stuff. Actually I was kind of an introverted, sedentary sort of person at the time. I remember there was a film class that I took, but I didn't make it through, because one of the requirements was to go down to the city twice a week to see a foreign film and report on it and it was just too much trouble. It wasn't so great going downtown, I was very content with who I was and my limited universe was fine, which was very, very abstract, but it was fine. I was doing a lot of sculpting at the time, a lot of painting. It encompassed 99 per cent of my time probably.

Just the thing about sitting in a movie theater didn't seem like there was any interaction there. One semester I completed, then went for another semester, didn't complete it.

My wife and I got involved in a relationship. My intention was always to go back to school, and possibly teach. I think I felt pretty strongly about that back then, about teaching; not so much of imparting the information of the academic world, but imparting a sense that life is really nice no matter what you did. Growing up I saw a lot of troubled people. Getting out of adolescence was a tough time for a lot of people. I helped a lot of my friends out, so I guess I analyzed that it would be nice to catch people at a certain age in an academic environment and not really be academic about it, just be life smart.

The relationship definitely became all consuming and you get into a world where you need money. This is immediate money, so I got involved in building. A few of the jobs weren't classic construction, definitely a deviation. It was appealing in the sense that it was different and I was starting to see. It had a lot to do with educating me as far as how things were put together and what could be done by people, by man. You know, somebody who doesn't understand that they have the ability, goes through their life not really seeing things. Like a house, all right it's a house but they have no conception. They're totally capable of putting a house together and therefore, they're totally capable of putting the Empire State Building together, and therefore they're totally capable of putting the Space Shuttle together, anything at all.

I enjoy building, even now. If I start a project, I enjoy finishing it. I was very much into living every day. I wouldn't look too much into the future. I lived every day. Everything about me was creativity. I needed that. Carpentry was a way to make money and possibly because it was a way to make money, that made it less than what it could be. For certain people, it can become more consuming and be a road to creation which I had no problem with; it's just that I didn't view it that way. My view of creativity was different. My view of creativity was what I had done in the past on paper and sculpture. It was "unique"; nobody had done it before. You try to see what makes who you are.

I came from a large family. There wasn't a lot of interaction; there was more interaction with the kids, brothers and sister than with my mother and father. My mother was a very, very affectionate woman, very kind, always reaffirming her love, the affirmative pat on the back at all times, always a knee to sit on. My father was just somebody to be feared, period--different school, old school. Grew up in "Hells Kitchen", was a bully. That has a lot to do with his mother and his father dying and being the only one to raise his brother. His mother died in a fire when he was about twelve.

I was pretty much left to my own, so you really had no direction other than the impetus that you got from your environment, not so much parental direction. Socially, I guess I was real adept because I had three brothers and sisters, so you try to fit into that framework. You understand complicated things in an abstract way to get along. I was the youngest for a long time so I adapted. I was the weird one. I remember that in school kids always used to pick on me. My father used to make me get these crew cut haircuts and I felt terribly self-conscious about them, because they made my ears very large and the kids picked on me and that used to get me so angry. A couple of times I blew up at them, but that made me more introverted.

When I was in sixth grade they had an art contest in the Catholic parochial school and I did a sculpture out of soap. I went home and I heard about the art contest and I brought it back the next day and the nun looked at it and wouldn't accept it because she didn't think I did it. So I went home and told my mother and she gave the appropriate response--she was very passive. She wouldn't fight. She said, "It's O.K.." At that point I understood that that was O.K., because there was some value to be gained. The fact is, I knew I did it, and I did it well and I did it so well that nobody thought I ever did it. So, that gave me a lot of understanding as far as internalizing this stuff. I didn't feel bad, I didn't feel hurt. I felt good, because I had proved something to myself. I proved that what I had done was good, unique and it was O.K. for people to make mistakes, because all that was really important was what was inside your head.

I was in church and they passed the plate out to give money. The plate had come around and I put some money in and this kid next to me...I don't know what made me notice, but this kid felt really bad that he had no money to put in the plate so I gave him some money to put in the plate and it made me feel real good. It made me understand that you can do things for other people to make their well-being better. Also I was inundated with a lot of the bible growing up in Catholic school, which I didn't pay too much attention to other than that the values there are good. You take care of your fellow man. It made a lot of sense not to be shortsighted and violent, all these stupid things that people do. Go after people, get your due if somebody does you. I'm a firm believer in turning the other cheek, setting a better example.

I started reading about theology, Calvinism, Gnosticism. It was a real desire to understand what mankind thought, not how we fit into, fed into everything--our concepts of God, how we created them, why we created them. I guess that's the point when I stopped going to church too. I saw church as a man-made contraption which had a very good place. I'm not disrespectful of it. People are the most important, that's all. Religion was made out of people. Immediately after that, I understood or respected every religion that ever was. All of a sudden it was very nice to be in the world. Before, you never even thought about it, you just were as a child with a lot of questions.

Somehow, something was filed for me and I got a notification to take the test. I remember going in, and the cops that were there to monitor it looked at me and said, "You want to be a cop?!" I looked very strange, I guess. I looked great as far as I was concerned. I wore an army shirt and hair down to my waist. I was smiling, calm, never spoke loud, anything you wanted to do...sure...pla, pla-pla, pla. And I took the test and six years later, I got notified that this was available and I thought strongly about a lot of things.

My brother who is different than I am was always into getting a job with the police department. He sort of got moved along on that track. Why he did it is his own reason. He sort of did what the masses do. He got moved along and found himself in that position, which is Ok, he's well suited for it. It had a lot to do with my father being a cop.

Growing up, there were certain things that I decided that I would not speak on, because I was not educated enough and I didn't want to put in the prescribed time to become knowledgeable enough to have an opinion on it, an educated opinion. Everything that I thought about, everything that I spoke of I felt strongly on, and had thought out. Politics was one of the areas that totally baffled me. There were certain topics in current societies that are important and consume a lot of time. Politics is one of them, and I did not like politics. I didn't understand politics and I really wanted to have nothing to do with it. But making that decision, I had a guilt because I'm a social being living in a society. I don't homestead. I don't live in the middle of nowhere where my environment is manipulated by me exclusively.

I am not the king so what I say is not law. I live in the framework of other people's laws and those laws are politics. That's the manifestation of politics for me. I had to become educated in the ways of politics or I had to move out of it, which is about the time that my wife and I discussed going to Alaska to get away. I was all ready. I was all ready to homestead. Everything I owned was in a backpack, except for my books. I'd have to send for my books.

So I try to find a rationale for doing it. Number one, it was so foreign to me that it amazed me that somebody was actually asking me to do this. I got the note and I say, "Holy shit, what the hell..." God, I tried to envision myself, experiment in actually being one, and it blew me away. The fact was that I understood that I was a human being that could do anything other human beings could do by virtue of the fact that I have the same appendages and the same brain. And it amazed me that I could actually just right now walk right into this, immediately walk right into it. Drastic, drastic change.

The family had nothing to do with it at that point. In the beginning they did when I took the test, but 5 or 6 years later down the road, no. So I wrestled with it for awhile. I really wasn't enjoying the carpentry anymore; bills had to be paid. Money was never an issue, but all the money we got went out to pay bills, food and stuff. It wasn't any stress or anything involved with that, maybe a little bit when I'd smoke a cigarette and I didn't have any cigarettes, and I went around the house collecting stuff out of the ashtrays.

So, I have a decision to make. One side of me says, "Wow!"; another side of me says "Don't do it" and another side of me says "Bernie", he says, "it's your answer to that political thing. This is your social responsibility fulfilled. What the hell, it's all an education. It's all a road to get somewhere." I didn't know anything about what I was getting myself into. I perceive from what I saw on the news at times and my limited interaction with police that this can't do anything but give me more data to paint with or to sculpt with or to create with or to write with. So based upon that, I subdued my fears or probably just didn't deal with them.

The money at the time was probably the same amount I was making as a carpenter, but I never realized that I made that much money. They gave me a dollar figure of an annual salary. I didn't know shit from shinolla about annual salaries. And it seemed ok, and we needed money. I had a kid, the family needed money. So there were a couple of reasons why: money, social responsibility, fear, dealing with that fear and the fact that I was totally, totally on the opposite side of the coin in terms of who I was and what I was doing at the time. So, I said "yes." I was game for anything. I've been game for anything all my life pretty much. I wanted stuff, not material stuff, I just wanted experience. So I took it, cut my hair, got a suit and went downtown.

This group that went into the academy was like, you know, the top of the class. It wasn't hard to become the top of the class, at all. I mean, you could not sleep for a week and still get in the high nineties on the tests that they gave. The people that got in there were not like me but were like my friends that I knew at the time. They were all like that. They all came from the drug era, the sixties, protests and stuff like that. Here they were and we sort of clicked. You know your little cliques that you get involved with? And a lot of them were good folks. So I liked that.

I've seen a lot of very strong stuff. I don't really remember the first day. I do remember the first time I, by myself as a police officer, was on a foot post, walking in the City of New York. They probably put me in the worst place on the planet. To this day, it's the worst place and they put me there by myself, they put me on a foot post in the worst possible housing projects on the face of the planet and said, "This is your post, we'll pick you up in 8 hours." I say "This is kidding me, right?" "Nope, this is where you're going to work." So me being the soldier that I am, got out of the car and did my job. And it went smoothly, went fine. A lot of fear, but I was always good at working things out in my head first, and I relied heavily on my ability to communicate verbally with people. And I did it well, and that gave me a certain amount of confidence. And extrapolate from that--if my mouth didn't work, I had a stick. The fact that I was going to hit somebody with a stick did not sit with me, but now I was dealing with the fear of getting out of there alive. There was my mouth, there was my stick, there was my gun in that order. And that was the rationalization, and it helped I guess. Maybe I should have turned around and walked away from it at that point. There's a lot of doubts.

I've seen a side of people that I wish I never saw. Society as a whole is removed from a lot of what happens in the inner cities. They get it via the media. I'm going to sound like I'm on a talk show now but to get it third party is much easier to digest than to get it firsthand, to actually walk onto a scene where somebody is taken apart, physically taken apart. You see blood, warm. Language is a poor excuse for communication. My chest is warm. My arms are warm, and I'm all red. I was covered with blood. That did something to me. Somebody was fatally stabbed and I was carrying him down to the street for an ambulance to come and get him.

The only thing that really has importance is your personal relationships, not the job. We constantly strive to do this, you know; we constantly strive to make them more personal, but it's not going to happen, 'cause management is doing it with the idea of raising productivity, by improving morale or whatever, but that's not the reason why it should be done. That has nothing to do with it; it's not increasing productivity, be it police work, be it hospitals, be it this or that. We're talking about the human condition and making them feel better has nothing to do with productivity at all. Productivity is not even...it's bullshit. Productivity is capitalism. It's finance. That has nothing to do with who human beings are.

I took the job for the adventure and I took it for the social payback. This was going to solve all my moral obligations for the rest of my life. The job, as I see it, is different than most people see it. On that job is this social obligation that you have; it's never changed, never has. Most people are not like that on that job. My social responsibility is to treat everybody the same. I never treat people like shit.

For thirteen years I'm working in the ghetto. Police officers that work in a ghetto start to see everybody as a criminal by virtue of the fact that so much is thrown at them, so much crime, so much of man's inhumanity to man is thrown at them that they can't believe it, so the defense is to get hard and to get rough and just "take care of it." If you commit a crime, we'll take you, that's it. The only problem is that a lot of people start seeing everybody as being the criminals when they're not, and they never have been. I always try to see the good that is in people.

When I first came onto the job, I was pleasant to the people that I arrested, until I changed at some point in my early police career when I sort of thought it out and decided that it would be better that I was not understanding and pleasant to people when I arrested them. These are criminals. This is not the people on the street. These are the people that I have arrested for crimes. I started to see a pattern in people getting locked up, and being thankful that you locked them up, because it's probably the best treatment they ever got or it's some sort of abstract parent to them. And it made no sense to make it appealing to them because they would come back, and if they came back they would eventually die in that system, either in jail or out in the street committing a crime. So the minute it dawned on me, I stopped giving them cigarettes, I stopped being their father. I stopped being their priest and I became a shit heel. I became a contrived son-of-a-bitch, on purpose. I was acting. I didn't like it because I didn't function well. I was not a very good shithead. I didn't know how to do it well, but I stopped being compassionate. Actually, I didn't stop being compassionate; I stopped outwardly expressing my compassion. I feel for these people. I feel for all of them, always have, inside. And if I see it coming to the surface, I just stop and don't do anything; I don't say anything. My compassion comes out for the victims a lot: women that get raped, people that experience a violent episode, either a spouse or a relative dying. With more of the serious stuff, you get a chance to express your compassion. I consciously did that in an effort to sway these people that I was coming into contact with, the criminals. "This is not a nice place, and you really shouldn't be here you know, please learn from it. Don't come back. There's nothing wrong with you that you can't stop doing what you're doing."

I view crime on a different level. If you're violating somebody, it's just not right. You got to make that decision. There are a lot of other nonsensical crimes that I have no view on. I had an argument with a lawyer about that, about the social ills of organized crime and the selling of narcotics, and marijuana. The crime that offshoots from that...I don't know, I'm a reasonable man. I'm receptive, I'm somewhat intelligent. I'm not the brightest guy in the world, but I'll be damned... I'm doing this for thirteen years and I see no correlation between the narcotics trade, and the robbery and homicide, other than the fact that some of the homicides are committed at the drug locations, the turf. But that's separate. I understand that aspect of it, but as far as the shit that goes on in the city, I can't see the connection. I mean the narcotics unit comes in and eradicates the narcotics trade in a given area, it doesn't eradicate the robberies; the robberies go up; the violent crime goes up. I'm supposed to see, and sometimes I feel inarticulate because I don't see it. I go to these meetings and I'm supposed to see it, but I don't see it. And everybody says that this is the reason why, and after awhile I say O.K., whatever you say. But I don't see that. What I see is totally different, it has to do with only one thing, morality. That's all it is. It's a problem with morality. It's a problem with parental interaction and the environment of adolescent people.

Interesting point in my life, getting a gun. I first remember feeling afraid of it, personally feeling fear and then within a very, very short period of time, I don't know how long, I felt dislike. It was a machine. I was very interested in machines, and how things work. It may have been hours, it may have been days after I got it, half of the fear went away. I honestly disliked it because it was so rudimentary. There was nothing to it but to kill people. I probably envisioned some sort of holy item that could do that. It should be complicated and beautiful, and it wasn't. My hammer was nicer than this thing. There was nothing amazing about it. It was a piece of fucking metal, that's all it was. I'm a very tactile person. I see beauty in the smallest things: pots, bark on a tree, even certain man-made things. But this thing had the equivalent appeal of a tire iron. There was nothing unique about it and it did so much devastation that I actually felt a strong disgust for it. So with that, it became very uncomfortable to wear, for whatever reason, I don't know why, it was uncomfortable for a long time. To this date, I guess, it's an adapted uncomfortableness. It's like my shoes. I wear it, that's all. I adapted to it. It's given no more concern than putting water in a glass, in putting change in your pocket. You know you're doing it and you have a slight subconscious thought about it that I could still recognize because it's different than anything else I do, but I do it so often now it's become very mundane. But I still recognize there's something different there. Strange enough, sometimes you don't feel right if you don't have it.

I use my gun all the time, a stop sign. There's been a couple of incidents where I've been fired at, and I didn't return fire. And surprisingly enough I was not frightened, not at all. Matter of fact, I was probably never sharper as at those moments. I became very methodical and mechanical and I knew everything that was happening. I saw everything. There was no fog or haze in either thinking or perception or my sight. Thinking about it afterwards, the process of it, I was thinking very tactically: where I was, was I going to get shot, where should I be if I have to shoot, all that stuff. Thinking about it afterwards, what I deduced was the fact that it is extremely difficult for me to shoot another human being no matter what. I will go as far as I have to go not to do that. Luckily the circumstances I was involved with, the quote, "termination stage," was never really reached, termination meaning firing to stop somebody. Other people that were around me fired and I can't be judgmental against them, because I'm not them. And I don't know what went on inside of their minds, but I do question it sometimes.

I got insulted once. Somebody fired a shotgun in my direction. I was chasing him, it was a car chase, me and my partner. Somebody had spotted the guy and they were following him and they threw something out of the window and they lost them. I was driving south on this road and I saw in the corner of my eye a car go by. I got the general color, like in a tenth of a second, so I turned the car around and immediately went in the general direction where he was going. All of a sudden, low and behold, that was the car they were chasing. In the middle of this chase, a passenger climbs out and sits on the window of the car and takes the shotgun and was about to shoot it at me. Survival instinct mandated that I turn the car. As soon as I turned the car and he turned the corner, I pursued him again and we got into a very big chase and it ended up that they stopped the car. Some of the police officers were chasing them on foot and they turned and fired. I jumped back in the car and came around him, and I found myself yelling. I got highly insulted that this person actually did this. I got angry. I learned an important lesson that night. I was about 6 feet from him and he still has the shotgun. I'm in the car with the window down and the guy that's in the car with me says afterwards, in retrospect, he says "What the hell is the matter with you? You didn't have your gun out. You were yelling at him; you were cursing at him. You were cursing and yelling at him, as you were pulling up alongside of him to get out of the car, and all he had to do was turn around and shoot you." And it never dawned on me. I got mad. My thought was not to kill him, I got mad. And I yelled, and I yelled, and I yelled.

He got shot. He got shot by somebody else, one of the cops. He lost an eye. He got shot in his eye while I'm yelling at him. I didn't know he got shot. It was like National Geographic. I'm not being cold or anything; I remember seeing National Geographic of an elephant getting shot, and lo and behold if that didn't flash through my mind when this guy went down. Certain images will stick with you forever; that's one of them. Another one was a very young pretty girl's eyes looking at me while she was dying. I guess there's a couple of others. I just can't remember them. I remember the strong ones.

I probably wouldn't have taken a job in law enforcement in a small town because of all the infamy that was attached to the large city, and policing in a large city. I was looking for input and data. If I was going to get data, I should do it in the place where it's most accessible and get the most amount of stuff that could be thrown at me. It was kind of naive of me to think that way, but it was good for that time. But I didn't realize how much would be thrown at me, and <u>what</u> would be thrown at me. I was a product of the late 50's, early 60's television; it was a buffer zone. There is no buffer, really. It's real life. It's like the flood gates opening up and here you are. I always remember, this is not life, this is a part of it.

I'm amazed that they glamorize in the movies what I do. It baffles me. It makes me laugh a little bit, gives me a bit of an ironic feeling that they immortalize what police officers do. They glamorize it and it's not glamorous, no shape or form. If you're doing it, it's not at all. It's a very tough job. My hats are off to the people who do it very well--and it's quite a few of them that do it very well. And the people that usually do it very well are the people who are ignorant or naive, people that don't think too much and my hat's off to them, immensely. I'm not saying ignorance in a condescending way. The phrase "ignorance is bliss" keeps coming back to my mind. I have met people that are ignorant and are extremely happy, and I can find no fault, no condescending thing about them at all; they are complete. And that sort of thing lends itself well to the extremes that are experienced as a police officer--don't think too much.

It's not all consuming. My whole thing is not money. In the past, it wasn't a concern, because I made the money and it went into the pipeline as they say. It's the same thing now. I had probably invested out of ignorance ten years of my life at this job, and I thought I just had to hold out for another five years and I was going to retire. Money became an issue, because you have to work to survive and that has a lot to do with the family, having children. My philosophy when I was young existed for Bernie and it was very simple, very complete. It changed when my own family came into play. I was not just performing for myself. I was performing for more than one and money was an issue. The plain fact of the matter is that other people had to be taken care of. I couldn't just live out of my knapsack anymore. So I changed. I changed to adapt to that and I didn't think about it, since I was in love. And love is blind, without a doubt. Not a cliché sort of thing, but you're no longer that self-indulgent.

You do feel good sometimes when you help people, an old person has a heart attack, you bring him back to life; that's a good feeling. Delivering a baby's a good feeling. You save somebody's life in some way, it's a good feeling. You give somebody directions, simple things, it's a good feeling sometimes. It's not a lot of things. It's like taking a line that's a mile long, maybe ten inches of that line are the good feelings, evenly spaced. When you first become a cop, there's more good feelings or maybe it's just that everything has changed and there's more resentment against the police. There's always a natural fear there for me too, against the police. From the outside looking in as just a normal person, if I get stopped by the police, the same normal things go through my mind at first, until I get a handle on it, and I do my professional courtesy thing and I say to myself, well, what am I doing? I <u>am</u> a cop.

Being a police officer is a very, very careful job. You have to walk on egg shells all the time, because simple everyday things that you might say are quite often misconstrued. You constantly have to be aware. Take a joke, "Why'd the Polish guy do this, why does the black person do this?" You could theoretically lose your job for saying something like that. That's extremely difficult to deal with. You find a lot of repression. Where it wasn't racism before, it becomes racist by virtue of the fact of that repression and the light that's put on it. It becomes an issue and it really shouldn't be an issue. You stop seeing people as people and you start seeing them as a guidepost as to how you can conduct yourself. If that guide is this person's color, you got a problem. That should not be an issue. It became an issue, and it's racism--created. It festers, it grows. There's a lot more now. It's difficult being careful.

They have to protect these people, they have to protect the police. It's their children--society's children. You're mandating them to do something, to take care of your society. You can't bang them around. You got to look at them, and you have to treat them with kid gloves. And, yes, there is a higher expectation there, but leave it as an expectation, not a dream list. They're asking for a dream list that is never ever going to exist and the results of that shit is devastating. It hurts society, hurts the police, hurts everybody.

I protect police officers, primarily. I protect my bosses and I lock up the bad guys. I cover all the bases on jobs. I'm very much into being self-sufficient and it relates through my police work. I take exception with making mistakes and leaving things undone. I don't like that, so I do very thorough work, sometimes to the point where I'm relentless in my thoroughness and people have difficulty with it. However, there's not a boss on that job that has any interaction with me that does not appreciate my input. You're not only trying to do your job but you're also trying to stay out of jail, everyday. No joking around. And as a supervisor, you're trying to keep your cops out of jail--everyday. And not all of them understand. If you understand the whole system and see all the pitfalls, it can become very nerve-wracking with the possibilities of what could happen in any given instance.

I'm very fatherly to my cops; sometimes they don't always appreciate it. I haven't seen any bad police so therefore, they deserve my undivided attention. They are human beings with good hearts and sometimes they need somebody to watch over them. And I watch over them as best I can at all times. I've seen people make mistakes, and bad things happened when actually that was not the intention. I have no problem with that.

I'm not a violent person and in the course of my doing police work, I have physically damaged some people, unnecessarily so. No way I could have gotten around it other than walking away and at that point I could have been arrested for not doing my job. And the moral imperative is that you're getting paid to do the job and the job is to protect society, lock up the violent people, the bad people. Everybody's good and bad, and under the same exact circumstances as I have experienced, cops have gotten prosecuted and it physically ruined them, mentally ruined them, probably for a long, long time.

I have no respect for the media at all. I've lost it. I never had a view on it before becoming a police officer. As a police officer, I have a view on it because I see it firsthand, the things that they report inaccurately and don't care about. It's just put the paper out, get it out, get the story out and sound intelligent. People eat this stuff up whether it's true or not. That's wrong, that's morally wrong. It's morally wrong because people take it as being the truth, and they know it isn't. Then it creates public opinion. That should be our politics, the newspapers. The papers should be written by the politicians.

Into It

Felice
Modern Ballet Dancer

I remember when I was really little, I was in a ballet class and the teacher went down the line, down the little bar and said, "Ok, what do you want to do?" And this one--"I want to be a doctor," "I want to be a lawyer," "I want to be a nurse." I said, "I want to be a dancer," and she was like--poof--"Well, we'll see." So now, it's like well yea, we <u>will</u> see. Because I <u>am</u> a dancer and that's that. I forgot about that for a little while and I wasn't sure, but deep down inside I really think I don't

We met for the interview in one of Alvin Ailey's rehearsal studios where Felice had been practicing. The Ailey Theater company graciously offered to accommodate me, an unpublished author – so like them to be open and considerate of a beginner. Perhaps also they liked my request NOT to interview a star, but an inspired beginner.

know what I would do if I wasn't dancing. I can't imagine people who don't dance. It's such a great thing, incredible to do.

I wasn't always dedicated to dance. When I was in High School, I was on the gymnastics team and the swim team and I played baseball, and everything that I did, I did but not great. Then after High School I decided, ok, now this is my chance to really concentrate on one thing. So ever since High School, and for the last three years everyday, I've been dancing and I haven't stopped.

It's more work than you will ever know. It's really physical and it's emotional. It's mental, it's cerebral, it's like everything. For a performance where you're going to do four or five pieces, let's say you've rehearsed for about four to five hours every day Monday through Friday, sometimes weekends if it's necessary. You've learned four or five pieces in a night from video tape and you go in and you rehearse them. Sometimes a choreographer comes in and they teach you and they're choreographing as you're in the studio, but it takes many hours and days and it's usually packed in. It's not like you have three months to do a performance of four or six pieces. You have like a month or two to do all that work.

I got this job working in this company and we were on our way to go to St. Louis, and I had to learn this piece. At the time I was living with my parents and my brother had this VCR in his bedroom, and I learned this piece which was about twenty minutes long in his bedroom. I was fighting the clothes that were hanging out of the drawers and the dumbbells all over the place and the surfboard that's falling off the ceiling and I'm kicking the walls, crashing into the armoire and stuff, learning this piece.

You press the VCR and you look at it and you say, O.K., O.K., that's a this, that's a this, and you stop the tape and you do it; O.K., I got that part, go on. Press the tape again, and you do the next phrase and then you stop the tape and you got it. Ok, it's in your head, it's in your head. Oh, missed that arm, got to go back, do it all over again. Or if you're in a studio and you learned it, there are tricks. You could put the television up to the mirror, and it's like you could just mimic. It's the opposite. The right arm is actually the left arm, but if you put it up to the mirror, it's the same way.

When I was very young, I didn't know very much about dance. I just knew that my mom danced. She went to ballet class and I used to play in her point shoes and put on her tutus, so I thought it was pretty and fun and so I went. Most children of that age do it because their parents send them.

I think the popularity has a lot to do with fairy tales and ballet in particular when you're young, that's what you usually start with. There's a princess and a prince, and there's love and flowers and a wicked queen or a bad man and the prince saves you. It's very "Brothers Grim." I think that's something that little girls see a lot in. They see the frilly little tutus and the pretty pink slippers and it's very glamorous, it's very "Romeo And Juliet," romantic. It could be just the same for a guy as it is for girls. They might have a very romantic notion, but most guys I know don't start until they're seventeen, eighteen and that is because they find that it's physical. It shows strength and it's challenging and it's a way to express themselves when in society, it's difficult for men to express themselves in certain ways. So they use dance to do it.

Dancers have a much different approach to the body than non-dancers, because they know what it's capable of and if they see a body they really like, it's like a work of art instead of just something to use or to give them pleasure or to stare at or gawk at or something. A dancer has a bigger understanding, a more intense understanding of the body and what it can do. They definitely see it differently. It's something to be taken care of, something to be cherished. I always say that this is all I have to work with. My body, my physical being is all I have in this whole entire world, so if I don't take care of it, if I don't use it to its fullest extent, I might as well not be alive. I could wear great clothes and I could sit behind a desk or I could do anything but this is really it, this flesh and stuff. This is all you have in the world, as far as I'm concerned.

You have to make sure that you're eating the proper foods. Like I'm dying for an Oreo cookie, ok? I walk into a store and I pass by the cookie section, but I say I can't do that, because if I do, then I'm ruining something that I'm working towards. That's one thing, food, nutrition and then another is keeping your mind clear of all things. You can't smoke, there's no drugs, there's no drinking. You have to get enough sleep and besides dancing, you should do a little more conditioning because your body gets very used to that. Get fresh air and I like to keep my mind going, as well. I'm not a college student or anything, so I like to read a lot and I feel that if your mind is clear and clean, then it takes care of your body. Go to the chiropractor every once in a while, get a massage, take a bath.

I'm a full-time student at the Alvin Ailey School. I'm a scholarship student. You take three classes every day plus any kind of rehearsals for workshops that are here. Six months ago, I was preparing for this performance that we had in the Cunningham studios downtown. I would have a 9 AM rehearsal, plus three classes during that day. I would have a rehearsal for another company from 4:30 PM until about 6:30. From 6:30 until about nine or ten, I would rehearse some more for this other company. So I was working with two companies, and I was taking classes.

In the media, I see these sitcoms on television and they represent the dance world as these crazy... I'm sitting with my roommates and we're watching these shows, and they're showing the dancers going out or sitting in California by the pool all day and then doing a performance. That's not really what dancers do. You don't go to a ball in a beautiful gown with diamonds. Dancers walk around in sweats all day, in sneakers. If you're not involved in trying to be a dancer, you have no idea what it's like. People think you just stare in front of the mirror and just jump around all day. I have friends who say, "Oh you dance, that's great! It's so cool, ah!" They don't understand. They think that I just get to dress up and wear makeup a lot and put on false eyelashes and go out to these parties.

Into It

My best friends are the people that I dance with. As far as a social life, you dance Monday through Friday, and then in order to live, you have to work. Well I do. The only chance that I have to make money is on Saturday and Sunday so I work in a store. If I want to survive, I have to work which means I rarely go out on Friday or Saturday night. And this has been going on for the last few years, because you need to be up, you need to be at work so you can go to school, and you can go to dance on Monday.

I had a boyfriend, but because I was so involved with what I had to do I couldn't have a relationship because it was always about, "Well, when I have time for you, that's ok, but if you're really about me, I have to get my career going." I could have had the relationship, but it had to be really light, like ok, you've reached me, ok, let's do something. But he couldn't handle it, because I couldn't give. I was giving so much to my dancing, to my classes, not even on such a big level to my career. It's just in my classes I was giving so much to what I had to do that by the time it came down to him, I couldn't give anything. There was this line that I couldn't cross because if I did, then I wouldn't be focusing on myself and that's basically what you have to do. That's why relationships are really hard. Most dancers I know don't have boy friends and if they do it's always a tug of war, like "I need your attention," "but I can't give you my attention."

When you're in a dance class there's a lot of emotions. There's a lot of insecurities that are being exposed, because you're learning something or you're doing something that you are not necessarily going to get quickly. It's takes time to learn and it takes a lot of practice and guts and a lot of strength and not a lot of people are on the same level. And then you feel this disappointment and you show this disappointment, and people feel it around you, and there's like all this emotion and energy. If you're in a classroom with the same people three times a day, five days a week, fifty-two weeks out of the year, then you get to know them, and you're going to really understand them much better than if you were in an office or college situation, because dancing is about exposing what's on the inside and bringing it out.

You have to fight everything; fight fear, fight the weakness. It's stubbornness. It's the fight against the body, a fight against insecurity. It's a fight against your mind. Like, oh, you'll never get this, you don't have the right body for it, you suck! And you're like, No, I <u>don't</u> suck. I'm going to do this! I'm going to get this. I'm going to stay on my leg. I'm going to turn out, I'm going to get my legs up and just fight it.

I always say that dance is too hard, so if you don't really want to do it and you don't really love it, then don't do it. You can't do it halfway, you have to do it all the way, because it's so hard and so demanding. It constantly needs your attention. I don't know what about it makes it so needy, like I need this from you. Like the whole world of dance is like I need you. I need all your time and all your attention. Insatiable, constantly. Everyday is like Tuesday. That's how I think. Everyday could be Monday. Everyday could be Wednesday; it doesn't matter because I work every day. For me, it's just constantly going.

Life is only a bitch if you make it that way. I'm very happy with what I do. The only thing that would make me unhappy is if I can't do something, if I try to do something and I'm disappointed in myself. That's the only thing that makes me unhappy are things that I control. It's this feeling, like you're just "in it" like you're _in_ it when you dance.

I love movement, being in control of my body and making it do things that I see and are incredible, and I love the music. I feel that movement and music together are very powerful. And then there's the theatrical aspect of it. I love being on stage, I like performing. I like being a ham. I love the dedication and I love putting a lot of hard work into something and seeing it pay off. It's so gratifying to say, "Ok, I'm going to do something, I'm going to work hard towards something," and then actually see it happen.

If you go into any other field, you'll be good at it because you already have this discipline ingrained in you. Discipline is doing what you have to do and really doing it. It's a fight and it's a struggle sometimes. I get up everyday and say, "I'm so tired, I don't want to go to class. I don't want to get out of bed. I don't want to do anything. I just want to sit here all day." My muscles hurt, but you get up and do it just like something you don't even think about. As much as you complain, you know five minutes later you're going to take command and you're going to go to class. And that's what discipline is. Doesn't matter what you want, you just do it.

My parents are very supportive. They're great, but they didn't teach me to be disciplined. That's something that you decide. Even my friends know where I'm going to be all the time. They know that I'm going to be in class. If I miss a class, they're like, "Oh my God, she missed a class!" I know what I want and I know that I'm not giving myself anything to fall back on. You know, they say dancers should have something to fall back on. I'm not thinking about that. I want to be a professional artist. I want to be in this field, so I'm just going to do what I have to do to get it. I'm going to work as hard as I have to and be as disciplined as I have to to be a dancer.

My dad was very artistic when he was young, but he quit. He didn't feel like doing it. Not that he's a failure or that I'm not proud of him in any way; it's just that he had this artistic ability and he did very artistic things. He was very talented. He doesn't like to talk about it a lot. He's very quiet, very mellow, very introverted. My mom is totally opposite. She's crazy, she's loud, she likes to go out. She thinks she's sixteen. She's really fun and she's my best friend, but she's not that deep. She's not really into anything. In other words, she didn't teach me the discipline either. Maybe they did in that they did what they had to do for their children, but not for themselves. They always did what they had to do.

I did gymnastics for six years from Junior High School through High School. Something happened in gymnastics that kind of helped me define what I do now. I was in a County meet, doing a floor routine and in my first tumbling pass I was so over-energized, I went off the mat and I was really pissed. Because I was so angry, I did the rest of the floor routine so energized and so full out, like I exploded. Like all this energy came out and I won. I came in first place and the whole time I was like, Man, I've lost, I blew it, I finked. Ever since then, I've realized what it means to have that and that's powerful. That's very, very strong and the feeling is something that I carry with me when I dance. It really had nothing to do with dance. It was an anger then but now it's like, "Let's see what you've got. Let's see what you've been working towards--to do what you have to do."

I didn't always know about dance. I knew that I wanted to dance, but I didn't realize that you don't have to be a ballerina to dance. You could be a dancer and do anything. I was always taking class, but at that time I didn't realize what it took to be a dancer. It's not like taking three ballet classes a night in a little studio. I didn't realize until after I finished high school, that I could then concentrate on what I really had to do. So I guess I always knew, but I just didn't realize what I had to do to get there until I started, until I was really involved.

I went to this college in Philadelphia, and I didn't know modern dance existed. I thought you had to be a ballerina; that's all I knew. I went there for a year and I did everything. I was always rehearsing for something and also taking classes. I really dove into it. The Juniors and Seniors always had showcases, they always needed underclassmen to put on their choreography. And in the summer I didn't want to stop dancing, so I auditioned for the Ailey School and they gave me a scholarship so I stayed here. It was better anyway and it was in New York. It was more real. I was nineteen when I started. In college even if you're a dancer, it's still college. Here, it's like, "Wo!" You are training like an Olympic athlete. You _are_ an Olympic athlete. I personally feel that if you want to be a dancer, don't spend tuition to do it. It's wasting money, unless you go to like North Carolina School of The Arts which is one of the best performing arts schools in the world.

It's very personal. A lot of people here go to four years of college, then dance. With me, I decided that school will always be there, so if I want to go back to college I'll do it when I'm too old to dance, when my body can't handle it any more. I do have an advantage because I'm younger, but it all depends on the individual. It doesn't necessarily mean I'll be more successful or better, just more years to try.

Now that I have been at the school and I've been exposed to more things, I realize that it's not the only thing that I want to do. You do something long enough and you realize certain things about it and I realize that the Alvin Ailey American Dance Theater is not the only modern dance company in the whole entire world. I have seen a lot of different things and there are other things that I like. I want to dance with companies in Europe. I want to live in Europe.

When I first came to the school, I commuted for two years on The Long Island Railroad, an hour each way. I did that if I had a rehearsal 'till nine or ten o'clock at night. But I decided when I turned twenty-one, I wanted to be independent so a month before I turned twenty-one, I moved out and I now live in Manhattan. I work weekends and it pays my bills. If I need help I could always ask my parents, but I don't. I just don't spend money. If I was living at home, I could go out to eat or I could go shopping every once in a while. Now I have to pay rent and I have to eat, so I can't really go out and spend money on frivolous things. This is what I mean about being disciplined, about knowing where you're going and getting there and certain things that you have to sacrifice. If I was in a company that traveled a lot, then of course I would give up my apartment, but if it's two weeks here, another two weeks there, then I would probably hang on to it and just pay the rent.

Dancers get paid, like nothing. I'm in another company also and I get paid $125. a week for four hour rehearsals, five days a week. It's like not even making a living, it's nothing. Then I have a season, I'm dancing for a week, eight performances and I'm getting paid four hundred dollars. So it's not even like fifty dollars a performance. You work so hard. And I know you can never measure money to talent or to art. You can never put those two up against each other, because they don't go together--money and art. But you've worked so hard! I mean baby sitters make more money than dancers do! After a while, you just have to laugh at how much money you don't make. You've worked very hard physically; you are totally beating yourself up. See, this is where it might sound a little weird, because I don't feel like I'm not getting anything out of it, I'm getting a lot out of it otherwise I wouldn't do it. But I feel like as far as money is concerned, if you measure money to work, then we should be getting paid a lot of money, because we do a lot. But we're not and it's just because it's an art.

I hope I'm not a lonely old bag when I'm sixty. I definitely won't be dancing, definitely not. I mean, I don't want to be an old dancer, trying to be young. I do think about what I'm going to do when I can't dance anymore. I'll go back to school and I'll learn something new, and I'll just do that. I'll do what I have to do, to do what I have to do. Like if I can't afford to go to school, then I'll make money. As far as being sixty, I can't even imagine living that long. I didn't even think I'd make it to twenty-one! Life is so precious. I mean you have this life and you might as well do something with it, because you only live once. So do what you want and do it well. Like dancing. I want to dance, so go for it. Just go for it, because you don't want to have regrets. You don't want to look back on your life when you're older and think "God, I should have done that" in order to have meaning to life. That's how you're going to give it meaning, by filling up every day. First you have to learn the step, and then the emotion will come to you. So don't tell me what to do because I'll feel it anyway. If it's true, I'll feel it.

When you see dancers on stage smiling, it's because they're really happy inside; they really are. So what you see on stage is basically what it is. You're not being lied to, otherwise, the person wouldn't be good enough to be there. In order to be a dancer, you have to be honest. You have to be honest with the movement and with the emotion. You wouldn't get to that point in your dance career if you weren't. You wouldn't be right, so you wouldn't be there.

Everybody feels it but can't really put it into words. You watch something and you learn how to put it in your body, in your own muscles. That's part of being a dancer. It is very intellectual. You have to figure it out; you have to figure all right, well what's behind the movement? There are a lot of ways that we're taught. Like a teacher will describe if your body has to be a certain way, they'll describe an hour glass. Ok your body has to feel like an hour glass or feel like you're scooping ice cream. So that to us is an intellectual kind of thing. You have to see the movement and say ok, how can I make that real? How can I make that really work? See what it looks like to you in life and then use it. If it looks like somebody wiping their hands through satin, then think of it when you do that. Think of wiping your hands with satin. Or if it looks like somebody's wading their foot in water, then that's what you're doing when you do that movement. That's what you're actually doing. You're wading in the water. Dance is such an "in the moment thing." At that moment you have to know.

There's this thing that dancers are dumb, but they're really not. They're just really very concentrated, very focused. You can't be dizzy or dazed or confused. You have to be on it. You have to be quick and sharp and be able to take things in really quickly. If you're not thinking, you can forget a routine. You always have to be thinking and totally focused. You have to know where your body is, your leg, and your arms are here. Your muscles react to what your mind is saying, so if you're not thinking, and if one move is kind of like another move in a different routine, you could backtrack. And I've done that. "Oh my god! I just did the other routine. It's a lot of focus. Your mind is always working.

I've had problems with being short before. I've had problems with a ballet company that I was auditioning for. I put on my résumé that I'm 5'2" but I'm like 5'1 & 1/2", and I'm petite. It's not just being short; I'm also like little, and I was auditioning and the girls are all tall and thin, very Balanchine. And then here comes me, little short me. But I don't move short. On stage, I don't look short because as a short person will know, you have to be big. You have to move big. You have to stretch. And I don't mean stretch your leg. I mean stretch the movement out, make it very long and lasting. I didn't lose this job, but the artistic director said I was just too short for her company, and my butt was not big enough. It was like the running joke with my friends that my butt's not big enough, and that I'm too short for this company. And all this time, I could have been eating donuts and she would have liked me!

Artistic directors have visions of what they want and if they don't see that vision, then you don't fit it and she was trying to replace this woman who is very curvy and very sensual. I can play sensual; I can be that because as dancers this is what you learn. You learn how to be honest within these roles, and I could be that. I am sensual and I could totally believe in that. If I was trying to be a ballet dancer in Balanchine's day, I would have never made it, never. I mean, you <u>had</u> to be tall and really skinny. But within this world, you can be anything. What's so beautiful about it is that it doesn't matter what you look like; it's what starts inside that you bring out; that's what counts. Things have changed and are still changing, still being learned.

You have to be, not crazy, but confident. Not even confident, 'cause I know a lot of people that aren't confident. I don't know what you have to be. I don't know if there's a word to describe what you have to be in this life. Maybe it is a little nuts, maybe that's what it is. I guess, if you're talking to a regular person, they'd say you have to be crazy not to have a social life, not to be able to go out, not be able to eat what you want, not be able to live like a regular person. And I totally feel like I'm not a regular person. It's always like us and them. They're regular people. I don't know what we are; we're like the aliens. And that's how we see ourselves. It's how a lot of dancers see themselves. People that you see on the street are dressed in normal clothes. Like we wear sweats and sneakers all day, and sweaty tee shirts and the people that are in their suits and in their nice dresses and their heels, like the people I saw on the train every morning when I used to commute; those are real people. Those are regular people. I don't know where I come from; I come from Mars or something! That's the mentality and it's not sad or anything. It's like a joke, like people would gawk at me.

I was going on the train, the Wall Street hour and I was in jeans and sneakers. I was in my ripped jeans, my tee shirt and I had just rolled out of bed and I had my coffee, like leave me alone! And it was funny seeing these women with their makeup on, the men in their ties and they'd fold their jackets, and put it on the seat. I always felt like this even when I was in school, when I was younger. Because of this dancing thing, I always felt like the outsider like I had someplace to go at night. I had to go to class and my friends were sitting outside and playing cards or doing whatever. So I always felt I had a life with them, but I also had this other thing that made me kind of not part of that. It's that discipline again.

I love my brother to death; he's really a good kid. For a little while, we were at that stage where I couldn't stand him and I just ignored him, 'cause I'd rather ignore him than be mad at him. Then I got to like him, and now we're friends. But he's leaving for school. He was a gymnast as well, and he likes golf. Golf is so boring. He's like a little stud. He's adorable and he knows it. He's got a great heart. He's a really good kid. He's not as dedicated to what he does as I am. Like I asked him last time I was home, so what are you going to do when you get to school? Like I think everybody has their life planned out in front of them like I do. He said, "I don't know what I want to do. I'll just, you know, go to school." I said, don't you know what you want to do for the rest of your life? Don't you know what you want to study? Don't you know what you want to be? He's like, "No, that's why I'm going to school, to find out." I'm like "Oh, ok." He's like "God, leave me alone already."

I don't want to sound like a total flake, but I feel like I'm not a grounded person. I feel like I'm an air person. I'm in the air somewhere. I'm not too deep with anything. I'm not too rooted into anything. You know, some people are very grounded and heavy, and I feel like I'm in the air floating all over the place, even when I deal with people, like my relationships, like my boyfriend. I wasn't very serious like "I'm in <u>love</u> with you." I was light. Everything was very light. The only thing that's not light in my life is my dancing. If I didn't have dancing, I would probably be like floating all over the place.

My philosophy is--do whatever makes you happy; just do it great; do it the best. It doesn't matter what you do; it's your life. I believe that everyone should live their life and learn from their own mistakes, not from other people's mistakes. But you have to be really honest and just go for it. And if you don't really want it, then don't do it because life is too short and it's too difficult.

Into It

To find out if you really want to be a dancer, you could take a dance class, and see if you like sweating a lot, and hurting a lot, and being yelled at, and told that you're too heavy, and too short, things like that--if you can take abuse. In all seriousness though, you don't have to give up your whole life in the very first days that you decide to be a dancer. It's something that you build up, something that you learn to love, or some people learn to love. And some people already have the love inside them.

Floyd
Musician/Producer

I'm not a songwriter by any means. I write songs, but I'm not a songwriter. What I do is I make music; I'm good at doing music. I'll come up with chords and some kind of musical structure, and usually collaborate with somebody who's good at writing to add the melody and lyrics. Sometimes I've done the melody and lyrics myself, but I never write from that end. I

always write from the technical aspect of--here's a musical idea, there's a bass line and a keyboard part and a drum beat, then here's something that sounds like a song. I'll collaborate with somebody who can hear a melody and lyrics for that song.

I can read music, but just barely. When I was young, I thought that was a big problem, but most of the work I've ever done was intuitive or it was like, here's the chord changes; it's a C and you draw the letter C and you knew that was the chord to play, and there was one measure, so you knew how many beats it was. If you can read music, there's a whole other level of work that you can do. If you are a musician and you read well, you can pursue being a studio musician. You can make a lot of money going into a recording studio, sitting down in front of a piece of music and playing it. I could never do that, could never think it out that fast. So, I can read checks, but I can't read music. I can read contracts; that's more important.

I'm into the sound of things. I don't know much about theory. I'm a good musician, but I'm good intuitively. I don't know a key the song is in sometimes. I don't pay attention to what the chords are. I just play whatever I feel, and start to structure it in my sequencer and the next thing I know, I've got a full blown song that just needs a melody and lyrics. And pop music is based on a lot of what the beat is and how things feel and the color of it.

I wrote my first song when I was 5, "Don't Cry On Me I'm Not A Handkerchief." It was sort of a list of things that I wasn't, something like that, like Mozart! I took piano lessons various times, from probably the age of 8 or 9 to when I was about 13, and I always hated it. Instead of doing my scales, I was making up songs. My last teacher was good, he gave me a much larger view of things. He taught me how to conduct. He taught me about orchestration, and other aspects of music, besides just playing scales and Beethoven concertos, which I actually got to.

I was never very formal about music. My parents were always cautious about that, because it's a tough business. My father knows firsthand, so by the time I finished high school my parents wanted me to go to college and study music education. They wanted me to prepare to fail, as I saw it. They wanted me to have a career to fall back on, to go to school, learn how to be a teacher. And I didn't do that; I joined a band instead at about seventeen or eighteen.

When I was thirteen, I knew I was either going to be a puppeteer or a musician. I was a puppeteer when I was a kid; I didn't make a living, but I made money doing it. I did puppet shows for the schools and got paid. When I was in sixth grade, I was doing puppet shows for the seventh graders and I had a stage, marionettes, hand puppets, and a little record player, and I was real good at it. When I got to be about fourteen or something, I found that I could make money doing shows, but I met more girls playing with a band, so it was an easy choice.

Most people I know wanted to be in bands to get girls. Some of them also, were interested in their instruments and wanted to make music. I was always into music. Since I was playing the piano and I was into writing songs, it was a logical place for me to be. When you're a kid, you might want to be an astronaut or the President of The United States. My thing was to be a puppeteer or musician. I never wanted to be an astronaut or The President of The United States, two things which have not happened so, you see, I had some real sense of where I was going.

I joined this band and I left that band. I guess I was in a lot of different bands over those years. I've had other jobs too. I've had a job in an educational publishing company. I've had jobs to support me while I was trying to make my career do something. I did temp work on and off during the course of the first eight years of my so-called adult life or independent life. I got to travel a lot doing the Holiday Inn circuit. That was for about eight or nine months. You go to each hotel for like three weeks. You play six nights a week, five sets a night. It's a lot of work. It was an adventure, 'cause it was the first time I got to travel and make a living. I was making money doing what I wanted to do, sort of. And I was getting some discipline about it which I liked, and learning to turn it into a business. It was a very hard job. That was the first time I was making a salary as opposed to getting paid by the night, and by the show. Before that, you got paid per show. Sometimes you'd play four times in a month, or sometimes you'd play twelve times in a month.

Then I got to another band, "TS Monk," and we were on a major record label so we suddenly had money. We were recording, we were traveling. We went out on the road, and did a tour which was more different than anything I had done. It was done in a much more professional manner. Then I came back to New York again, and started doing studio work. This was the first time I had a real record out, a professional record on a real label that was distributed and got on the radio. After that, I stayed in New York. I stopped traveling. I had enough.

I found that I had developed a greater love than playing music, which was making records, much to my surprise. I could still be playing, but I wanted to have control over the process of making a record. I started slowly getting into that by finding groups that needed to go into the studio, but didn't have the starting point or didn't know how to go about doing it. And I was making money playing as a free lance musician, recording on people's records. In other words, I would get called to come in and do over-dubs, to add music parts, mostly synthesizer parts.

My main tool is the sequencer which is, actually, the computer software that organizes the music that we play on the keyboards into a song structure. It's taking sounds and musical parts and arranging them. It's like word processing, but with music. Like taking a story and re-editing it and shaping it and so on, but you're doing it with musical notes and sounds. If I went to a studio, and I had to bring only one tool with me, I would bring my computer sequencer.

Somebody has a record or a song finished, but they want some extra sounds, extra parts, things to enhance the record. I would get called in to do that. And I made a living at it. It was very sporadic, but it was enough to sort of survive. And then I just started doing more and more production work, and then somewhere about '84, I went to work for a small record label; it had its own recording studio. I became their in-house producer and I got paid a weekly salary to come in and work on records. I would also get bonuses and royalties on things, most of which never came to light. I didn't see most of the stuff that was promised to me, but I did get paid my salary, and I did get to learn how to work a recording studio.

So it was sort of an on-the-job training situation. I learned the technical aspects while I got to make records. From there on in I just started producing records, and that's what I have been doing ever since. I still work as a musician, sometimes, not playing on stage, but working on people's records. Between that and some of the production work and the royalties which catch up with you after a while, you make a living.

Writing is a very lucrative thing, possibly more lucrative than being a musician these days. The royalties become very important. That's where most people make their money, or they make money on their advances and their fees. Royalties are important because they accumulate over time and you may have a period where things are slow, but there's a royalty check coming. I've had lots of periods where I've been carried over by my royalties.

Royalty payments happen when a record company sells a certain number of copies, and you have some percentage of the sales of that record or percentage of the writing of it, and then you get money based on how many times it gets played on the radio. Writers also get royalties based on record sales. If a record sells a hundred thousand, the writer gets a certain percentage based on that.

A general percentage that's usually accepted as a producer's percentage is three percent. That means the producer of the record gets three percent of the selling price of a record which is not very much. There are standards in the music business, and then lawyers fine-tune those standards. Once the record is broken down, everybody gets a small piece. The record companies get the biggest piece. However, a record that sells a lot can make a lot of money and that three percent can suddenly be worth a lot of money. Some producers get five percent, depending on what your value is in the industry, how important you've become. That's why song writing is a very lucrative thing, because song writers don't get advances, but they start collecting royalties the minute a record starts selling or gets air play.

Technology has changed the industry radically. People are making records in their living rooms now. Previously you had to spend a lot of money, a hundred dollars an hour or more to go into a professional recording studio and make a record. But now, technology has become affordable, and the quality is exceptional and people are buying equipment for a fraction of the cost of a professional studio, and making their own records. I've done this myself a few times. That's an interesting sort of investment. It depends on the kind of music you're doing too. You're not going to record an orchestra in your living room, but if you're recording popular music, there's a lot of ways of cutting costs these days by doing things yourself. There are a lot of scaled down studios that can get pretty amazing sound and be competitive.

I have a small studio space. People will come in, and they have a song, and they want to make a tape of the song, more than just a piano and a vocal. They want it to sound like an orchestra or like a full band. They want it to sound competitive with the music that they're hearing on the radio. I can make a scaled down tape that sounds competitive; I can make an impressive model that they can then take to a record company to try to get the funding to then go into a real studio and make a bigger record. In the meantime, I'm getting paid for my work to make that demonstration tape, and if they do get a record deal or they're going into a bigger studio to make it, I usually get hired to do that work as well, because I've laid the groundwork, and I can take that groundwork with me and then enhance it in a bigger setting.

I've tried to set my own standards. One of the hardest things about being self-employed is structure, making a schedule and making rules about your structure. I mean, I have this studio space and I always have friends who have a great song. "Let me come in and work on this song and then we'll sell it to a record company, and we'll make a lot of money." When I was younger, I would do that sometimes, but now I have rules that anybody who comes into my studio to work, has to pay for the time. For one thing, you start to realize that no matter how talented someone is or how good they are, there's a million aspects to what makes someone a success in any industry. You have to take <u>calculated</u> gambles if you want to eat and pay your rent. You can't just gamble all the time; you have to balance it. You're also trying to be a company. You're a sole individual, and you're trying to be boss and the employee and control all the aspects of something. It's not enough to just be creative, and know how to work the musical equipment, or the recording equipment. You have to also know how to be a businessman.

When I was growing up as a musician, like in the seventies, the concept was you're a musician, you're supposed to think about your music; you weren't a businessman. That was the popular notion. You just played your guitar, man. Now, the world is different, the business is different and my situation is different, and you start to think, "I have to make my own schedule, or there'll be no schedule." I have to set rules and standards, or there'll be no standards.

In the seventies, it was very artist oriented. Everybody wanted to be creative, and the record companies were catering to the creative aspect of things. Now, it's a business. In those days, it was run by people who loved music, and wanted to hang out with the rock stars. Now, it's run by lawyers and accountants, except that the lawyers and the accountants now have an ear, and also want to hang out with the musicians.

In some ways, not always, it's a better business; it's run more efficiently. But they are lawyers, they've got degrees, they know their business first. And it is a business, so you have to have a sense of what that business is that you're taking on. You can't just step out the door and say, "I'm a great songwriter, therefore, I will have a career." Or "I'm a great singer, therefore I will have a career." It's like, "I'm a great singer, now I need to have my business together." You need to either be able to represent yourself well and promote what you do well, or you need a manager to do something like that.

A lot of people may be good singers, but they don't know where to start. They don't know how to shift, to sell themselves in a conversation which will get somebody to then spend time with them and hear their tape. You have to get to the record companies, 'cause that's the center of the whole thing. There's a lot of ways to do that. First of all, there's access. If you live outside of New York or Los Angeles or Nashville, you've got a lot of challenges. If you're going to deal from that point of view, you have to deal with the mail, and that's a rough one. Record companies get thousands of tapes in the mail. They have departments called A&R Departments that are designed to listen to those tapes, and sometimes it will take months before they get to your tape. Sometimes they never do; it gets lost in the shuffle.

But there's a lot of music coming out of smaller towns in other areas, and even though the business is located in three or four main places, I think that you could be almost anywhere now and start to pursue a career. You could be a songwriter in Des Moines, and make your tapes and get them to just 2 or 3 people in New York who react to them and start to build something, because of the technology being more affordable, and there are recording studios on different levels everywhere.

The first thing to do is to try. Everybody has got to come from somewhere. All these bands have to come from somewhere. More often than not groups get signed, because they have connections in the first place. They hooked up with a manager who also manages a group on a certain label. He can then walk their tape into that label. Or they're playing in a club in Michigan or something, and somebody hears them and talks about them and writes them up in a local column which intrigues somebody else, who tells somebody at a record label. There are a lot of ways, indirect routes to getting heard, or building up a fan base in a certain area. You could be playing in Seattle and get good reviews, and build up fans who come to all your shows and then contact record companies and send them a package with your press clippings, showing that you exist and that there are people who are already in tune with what you are doing.

I was a manager for several years. I managed Nosara, a singer. I shopped her tape around to record labels, got her a record deal and took over the business aspects of things, the day-to-day dealings with the record label, the booking agent and after a couple of months, I also took on a second singer, as well. It was an impossible time, because I was spending all my days doing business and all my evenings trying to make music. I found that those are two full-time jobs, and I couldn't do them both at the same time. Managing is more lucrative, because I was making a percentage of the people I was representing, and they were both working. I eventually made a choice. I said what I really want to do is to make records and do my music, so I gave up the managing.

Managing is a full-time job and at its best, it's handling the details of things. At its worst, you can become the baby sitter for an artist, which a lot of managers are. That's something that was also popular in the seventies. Your manager was your baby sitter and nowadays, it's very different. Most artists, as they start to pursue a career in the music business, start learning about the business out of necessity. So the manager's concentration is more fine-tuning now; they're dealing with more specifics of the business, unless there are personal problems.

I've had a very up and down career. I've had some successes and some non-successes. There was a group I was in and we had a recording contract with Atlantic Records, and we had a record which was a modest hit single ("Give Me The Good Life") and got a lot of radio play. I didn't make any money from it. I got paid a flat fee to play on it, but it gave me some public awareness. I could talk to people and say, "Yes I worked on this record," and it got me some other jobs. That sort of started things.

I had other successes on that level. I worked for a group called "Kid Creole And The Coconuts" and played on one of their records which did ok here, but was a number one or two hit in England. Those were more psychological highs or successes. They felt good, but I wasn't making any money from them.

A number of years ago, I had a record that I produced and co-wrote, called "Summertime-Summertime." This was with Nosara, the singer I was also managing, and that record did very well and it made us a lot of money. We made money not just from radio play and sales, but we made money from live shows. She would perform the song, and I would make a percentage of that money. That was a more complicated situation, because we were a fifty-fifty partnership. It was unusual, because we were also involved in a personal relationship. I wasn't simply her manager and producer. That's pretty unusual. That's not the way things usually work.

A manager usually gets twenty percent of what an artist makes, sometimes fifteen, sometimes twenty-five, but the industry standard is twenty per cent. They're making twenty percent of the gross, so if an artist goes out and does a show and makes ten thousand dollars, the manager gets his two thousand dollars, and then the booking agency takes ten percent off the top to book the show and then from the balance, the artist has to pay for their expenses, any musicians and so on. So it trickles down very fast.

Recently, I worked on a film called "Juice" where I got paid a flat fee to play on some of the songs, and I also played on the sound track itself. But I also co-wrote one of the songs that was on the album, and so I will make money as a writer. I will see a royalty as a writer from that, and that song is also released as a single, so I will make money from that as a writer, as well.

I've had enough downs to balance out the ups. The most creative aspects in the music business are not salaried. You're paid for what you do, when you do it. If you're a musician and you're in a band, you get paid when you play or you get paid royalties, but there are very few salaried positions, unless you're doing something like the Holiday Inn tours. You get paid when you work. If you don't work for three weeks in a month, you don't get paid for those three weeks, unless you have royalties coming in from something that was out six months earlier, and it's now trickling in. The balance is that you can sometimes make a lot of money. You might make in one week what you need to pay your bills and rent for the period of a month. You don't have health coverage so if you want it, you have to get it. You don't have the benefits, you don't get paid vacations. You have to do these things on your own. I don't have health insurance right now. I've had it for the last five or six years, but I abandoned it a year and a half ago, 'cause it was just too expensive. It's something I need to do, but it's also on a list below paying rent and bills and eating. There's also certain expenses I have in maintaining my studio such as occasionally upgrading equipment.

I started to find that I wasn't enjoying myself all the time, because I was working all the time. And even though I love my work, I needed some distance from it. That's why I don't have equipment in my home. I don't have a keyboard in my home. When I come home, I have to read, or watch TV, or do something else. I cannot work. That's actually very important, to have this division of work and life.

Having the creative control over the aspects of making a record is my favorite thing in the world. A lot of the records I produce, I'm also playing on or involved in writing. Somebody has a song, an idea and for me to be able to give them some objectivity is a great thing; to have a perspective on something that exists already, and therefore to be able to step back from it a little bit is a great feeling. To me, the recording studio is my favorite place in the world. The technology and the trick of translating a song through the technology into a finished product is the most challenging and rewarding experience I know of outside of some more personal things which probably have nothing to do with this... It's just a great process.

Theoretically, the best producers don't have their identity on the record. They're supposed to bring out the identity of the artist in the best way possible. That's a hard thing to do, but that's the theoretical idea of a perfect producer. The line is very thin these days between producers and artists.

An artist may be somebody who writes a song, and also produces it in the studio. Or a producer may be playing on a record like I do, on the records I work on. I'm not just sitting there with the engineer trying to translate the singer's idea to tape as much as I may be also playing the keyboard parts or the drums or something. So there's a lot of thin lines now between what producers are and what artists are. The artists have the responsibility of having their picture on the record cover and going out on the road and promoting the record and those things don't interest me at all. I prefer being behind the scenes.

If somebody gets a record out, that's a major accomplishment in the world, 'cause there's so much competition. It's not enough to just get a record deal. You got to get your record made and get it out in the world. So a friend of mine recently got a record out, and it's a finished product, and it's in the record stores and that's what it is. For me to call up and say, "Listen, why did you do this, or you could have done that, or what's the story with this?" doesn't serve any purpose. I respect anybody who gets a record out in the first place. But not wanting to lie or anything, I'll find a diplomatic way of saying things.

There are producers who are known by people who buy their records because of their reputation of being a great producer, in which case, the singer becomes a piece of the producer's puzzle. Phil Spector is the one who took the producer out of being the invisible guy and into being a key player. He had a sound that he made famous, and people came to him to make that sound, to recreate that sound with different singers and different songs. That has a term called "wall of sound." He would make very dense sounding recordings and he was really stretching the limits of technology at the time.

The concept of a pop record is that it is a product; it's not just a song. Pop music, at least in the top 40 of radio, has always been like that. It's been a manufactured process which artists have sneaked through. A lot of popular records are made to be sellers. They're made with a certain formula in mind. This is the sound that's popular nowadays. This is the technology that's popular.

I'm in the popular music business. I'm not producing esoteric music; I'm producing commercially based music, but I'm not thinking about how I can make this more commercial. I have a project that I'm working on now, and a couple of people said to me, "Why don't you do it more like this, 'cause it'll make it easier to sell?" I'm not going to do that. It doesn't mean I won't on some things, but you have to have integrity about what you do. You also must not be a damn fool. Well, fuck what everybody else says; this is the way I'm doing it, unless that's the goal that you have--"I'm doing this entirely on my own terms and fuck the world." Then you'll get accepted or not accepted on those terms.

I'll turn on the radio, but it usually won't stay on more than about 45 seconds. I get things from word of mouth, or somebody will recommend something to me and I'll go out and buy the album. I'll see a video on MTV and I'll be intrigued and buy the album. Or I'll read 3 reviews in 3 different magazines raving about something. I'll check it out. So I try to keep up on things that way, but I find the radio impossible. I can't listen to it, 'cause I like rap music, but I like maybe 20 per cent of what I hear. So it's the same with the radio. If I put on a radio station, maybe they'll do one song in an hour that I think is good. I'd rather read a book, pick my nose or go into a coma.

The music business has become wide open and some people are threatened by it. You can be somebody who has no musical ability whatsoever, but you can buy equipment that will help you translate your ideas and if you've got good ideas, then more power to you. The world is glutted with guys who can play great scales on their guitars, but I'd rather have somebody come along who can't play all that well, but could put together a great song, or play three notes that were the right three notes.

Into It

Paul
Politician, Town Supervisor

I'm spending one day a month working in different departments. I've been a sanitation man for a day, picking up garbage. We don't pick up garbage in commercial property if it's over a certain amount of tons, but what happened is, we showed up and then we went back and we picked up the garbage 3 times in the same place. So we went back, and back, and back, and each time we were below the tonnage. Basically, the problem is the town would charge a commercial operation for the pickup of garbage, and some of them will go out of business. If they go out of business, our tax base is going to go nuts. Most people have told me to be reasonable. They say, "Think before you act." They said, You can't come off being hard. Let's say that I fired the sanitation people who would do that; they could become rude to the consumers, won't pick up the garbage and we'll have a deterioration of services. In fact, when I cut overtime about a month ago for about a week, there was a big slowdown.

I told the Commissioner of Sanitation what I saw and said let's look at the commercial garbage operation and see if we could reform it so we're not going to have this problem in the future. So I took action on my own, but I did not discipline these people. I want the whole larger system fixed up.

The second thing I did is I worked as a carpenter and we built four park benches on East Hartsdale Avenue. That was interesting actually 'cause the town carpenter is really from the old school and starts every day at 5 o'clock in the morning even though he doesn't have to be at work until 7. Just a really fascinating person. He loves his job so much, he comes in on weekends. He takes such pride in maintaining all the parks in the town.

The old school is somebody like the old fashioned doctor who would make house calls and who you see really cares; not in it just for

Paul is an idealist and a pragmatist – quite a combination for a politician. We met for the interview in a pizzeria in Hastings-on-Hudson, NY. The ambiance accommodated the interview and the interviewer perfectly.

the money, but generally loves his or her work. You know, like when you come to a restaurant and they mention your name. That's the old school, an old fashioned thing as a local home town touch and I guess pride. Like if there were complaints about any aspects of the park, he'll be upset for a week.

I also spent a day constructing or blacktopping sidewalks and it was interesting because the crew that I was on had to wait an hour for the blacktop so in the middle of our work, we had nothing to do for about an hour, so I'm meeting with the asphalt company and trying to get them to shape up and give us better service. And then I'm going to be a Park's Cash Attendant and a Police Officer, just going the regular beat. It's sort of interesting because when I was a legislator up until last year, I was dealing just with the public but here I'm the Town Supervisor, and an administrator and I have to supervise about 500 employees.

I'm the Greenburgh (NY) Town Supervisor. A supervisor is in effect like the mayor and administrator. It's the chief elected official for the Town. There's about 83,000 people. I have to supervise the Police, the sanitation people, recreation, the Water Department, the tax office, propose a budget, a whole bunch of things.

I feel that the job has 3 aspects. One is the administrative where you're managing and overseeing about 500 employees, and proposing budgets. You're the chief executive officer and a chief financial officer for the town. And we're one of the largest towns in the state. The second aspect of the job is really helping people with government red tape and constituent problems. If people have problems pertaining to the town, they call me and I try solving it. If they have problems pertaining to any other government department, whether it's federal government or a state or county, they usually call me and I'll try helping out also. The third is proposing laws and making recommendations to the council.

There are other aspects. For example, cutting ribbons, and campaigning. You have to run every other year, and going to dinners, giving out proclamations, making speeches and if somebody is honored, you know, by an organization, I may give them a scroll, saying "Whereas, whereas, be it resolved that today is Jennifer Smith Day." Then you make a speech saying how great they are. Going to a lot of meetings of community groups, answering a lot of letters, organizing agendas for meetings, presiding over a council, taking the heat from people who might be angry about something that you may not have any control over. For example, the county decided to establish a homeless shelter in the area with 116 single men, some who have come out of jail, so the neighborhood is upset. I was able to get the neighborhood to say we will accept 50, but they're blaming me. They're blaming the county and the town, anyone in government for hurting the quality of their life. I don't always have the control, but people don't understand the different layers of government.

The Town Council is like the Congress or Board. We have four council members and a supervisor. Each of us has one vote on the Council. I preside and in New York, the town form of government has generally, a weak supervisor so I can only appoint people if I get three votes of the council members. It's possible for three council people to band together and appoint or fire people when I disapprove. So it's sort of like a mayor, but a weaker form of mayor. The Councilmen are elected for 4 year terms and the Supervisor is elected for a 2 year term.

I was born in 1956, and lived in Westchester all my life. My parents live in Scarsdale. First I wanted to be a Rabbi, then I decided to go into politics, for the reason that I always wanted to help people. When I was growing up I felt that a Rabbi is somebody who helps people, one on one. And ideally, politicians should help people, but unlike clergy members, you could help millions of people or thousands of people with legislation through your offices. It's not just individual counseling. When I turned about 13, the Rabbi went on vacation during my Bar Mitzvah. The substitute Rabbi said, "Why would you want to be a Rabbi?" I sort of lost interest. He said, like you're crazy, this is a stupid job to be in.

Then I was walking downtown with my parents and we saw somebody handing out literature for Richard Ottinger. He was a congressman running for The United States Senate and my mother said, "Why don't you do something with your life?" So, we found out who our congressman was and it was Ogden Reed so I called his office and offered to volunteer. I was about 13. My parents only knew a little bit about him. He was the editor of the Herald Tribune which had gone out of business, and was Ambassador to Israel. I called the League of Women Voters, and found out who the Congressman was, and it was him.

I loved working in his office, not because of the politics, but because his was a really good campaign. Campaigns take any volunteers, you know, to stuff envelopes, make phone calls, lick stamps, collate. But what I liked about his campaign, which I thought was the most interesting thing, was in the back of the room. They had all these cakes and desserts, ice cream and sodas and junk food. My parents didn't encourage my sister and me to have cakes a lot so what I did is, I used to go there every day just for my dessert. It was really very exciting, you know, because you'd see him and the TV cameras and radios. He was somebody who at that point was being considered for Governor, so he was like a rising star.

A couple of years later, in 1971 or '72, I called the head of the County Democratic Party and decided to form The Young Democrat Teens of Westchester which became very successful. There was a woman who worked for Richard and she suggested that I attend meetings of the County Legislature rather than just work for candidates. She encouraged me to lobby for bikeways and bicycle paths. I lobbied for a $50,000. grant to build a bike way along the Bronx River Parkway and I went to every meeting of the County Legislature, circulated petitions, called all the legislators at home, late in the evening. And they got sick of me and finally the minority leader of the legislature went up to me and said, "I'll tell you what, we'll pass it and build a bikeway. We'll appropriate $50,000 provided you don't show up for 6 months at the County Legislature. So, I said ok and for 6 months they never saw me and we got the bikeways. This was in 1973 when I was sixteenish. I'm now thirty six.

Then I worked on a lot of different issues like getting the County to pass a Youth Advisory Council. I sued the County Legislature trying to get them to open their meetings to the public. Since I lived in Scarsdale, I also sued the Village of Scarsdale trying to get open meetings. There was a club in Scarsdale that excluded women as members; it was an all male club, one of the most prestigious clubs in the community. Over a thousand men belonged and they selected the mayor and Village Trustees for Scarsdale. They have a nonpartisan system where people run unopposed and are prohibited from expressing their views on issues until after the election. And they've been doing this for many years.

So I knocked on virtually every door in Scarsdale in 1976 and I organized a petition effort and we called the committee "The People For a Whole Town Club" because half the people couldn't join. There's a lot of Wall Street lawyers and business people, and really successful people who live in the village. In Scarsdale it was very popular to say, "I'm against having women as members," but then what we did is I contacted the National Organization For Women and we picketed every meeting for about a year. We had NBC and a lot of the TV stations at their meeting and they didn't expect it. So as people were voting, the cameras were shining and women were admitted. This won by 12 votes and the New York Times did an article in 1977, since it was such a significant issue.

The next thing I did was the busses. The trains to New York just weren't being run very well. The windows didn't open. The air conditioning motors broke down, it was over 110 degrees inside. There were frequent delays, so I decided that I want to organize some competition to the railroads. I organized a bus service. I handed out questionnaires at train stations asking if people wanted to secure a bus service to New York. The MTA called the police and threatened to have me arrested because I was starting a competition. So what happened was, I went to the Associated Press and they put it all over the wires. It got all this coverage, state-wide. The MTA about 2 days later, backed down, because I had the Civil Liberties Union represent me and made it a major case.

I was successful in starting an alternative to the railroad, and we had 3 busses leaving in the morning, and 3 in the evening from New York City and I did it as a volunteer. I made no profit. We just figured out how much a bus was going to cost and just charged passengers for the daily cost for a month. I did it for about 18 months out of my home but in the meantime, the county and the state, and the city were trying to undermine me. New York City kicked us off 5th and Madison Avenues. The County of Westchester kicked us off Central Avenue. The Village of Scarsdale kicked us off Gunermore Road and we ultimately were forced out of business. But when we did that it was sort of interesting, because then the county set up The Liberty Lines Bus Company, express busses to New York.

Then I thought that everybody knew me because I was like on page 1 of the Westchester Section of The New York Times. It was on Eye Witness News and all the major New York stations. I said, I'm going to run for State Assembly. This was ten years ago. So I announced my candidacy, knocked on about 3,000 doors. It was a redistricting year and about a month and a half later, the Justice Department eliminated all the districts, so I didn't run. It was aggravating. I practiced law for about a year; a little Real Estate, a little Commercial, a little Negligence--hated everything. I found it boring, tedious and I didn't get satisfaction representing people who I didn't agree with.

As a politician, you can pick and choose what you are going to do. As a lawyer you have to represent the people who pay you and you can't be picky, otherwise you're out of work. So, I decided to run for the County Legislature the following year against Tom Abonanti, who was then a four year Councilman and very popular. I just moved into the district, so I didn't really know much about him or the Mayor of Irvington. They were the people who I ran against. Tom really took my race as a joke because he figured I was a "political activist." All his friends were saying, "You're going to clobber Feiner." But I knocked on the door of everybody who votes in primaries and by the time he started campaigning about a month before the primary, I had met everybody. Also, Common Cause had given me one of 6 national awards for public service, for starting up the bus service. I won the primary and the election.

When I was running, people swore "We'll never see you again, just like all the politicians." And I said, "Yes you will, I'll be at the supermarket every week," because I stood in front of the Grand Union every day from May until November. My strategy was just to stand in front of the supermarkets and talk to people. And I might be the first candidate in The United States to have a money back guarantee on promises. I said if I ever break a promise, people will get their money back if they give a contribution. You know, everybody has always been sick of politicians and it was sort of a different approach and I wanted to convey the image that I'm not going to be the typical politician who says one thing and does the opposite once they're elected.

After I got elected, I wrote to the mayors of the villages asking if I could set up an office inside all of the village halls. The Villages of Hastings and Dobbs Ferry said no. I said, how will I stay in touch with them? People will forget who I am and I won't be able to keep my promise of being accessible. And in January, it's really cold out, so you can't stand outside the supermarket every week. So I wrote a letter to the heads of the Grand Union and A&P and they said, sure you could stay. And since then, I've been at the supermarkets every week for over 9 years now.

I basically set up a card table with a sign that says "Greenburgh Supervisor, Problem Solver," and I have a bunch of handouts that could be about voter registration, information about parks and veteran services, consumer information, and I give it out at the desk. But more importantly, I answer questions that people might have about government. And people who have problems, I'll try helping them. It's really the most rewarding aspect of the job.

The thing that I'm most proud of, there's a woman who passed away about 2 years ago. She was confined to a wheelchair, a juvenile diabetic, no use of her arms or legs, totally blind, and she called me up and said, "I don't want to go to a nursing home and the doctor said, I'm deteriorating so rapidly, I'll have to go. I want a home maker. I have a young daughter and I want her to be with me and I don't want her to remember me as somebody in a nursing home." I called Social Services and they said they wouldn't pay for it. When they denied it, I went to an Administrative Care office with her and argued and said this is terrible what you'd be doing. You're willing to pay for a nursing home but you're not willing to pay for a home maker. We were successful and got them to pay for it.

Later she calls me up with another problem and I said, I'll only help you on one condition, that you help me. She said, "How can I help you, I can't see, I can't write." I said, you're to go to my office. She said, "That's impossible, I'm going to be humiliated outside." I said, "Ok, see you, I won't talk to you." I said, "I'm telling you, I'm giving you 24 hours; you have to call me from a pay phone." She said, "Everyone is going to laugh at me, because everybody in town knew me as somebody healthy and vibrant. I don't want them to see me in a wheelchair." So I said, "Ok, then I'm never going to talk to you again."

So she calls me from a pay phone from the diner in town saying she was out and she was excited, like it was the greatest thing in the world that ever happened to her. So then I said, "Now you have to work in my office." "I can't do that" she said "Ok, see you." So then, she started going out and she loved it. I put her in charge of the homeless program in my office where she used to go to the homeless hotels, knock on doors, tell people that if they didn't get a job, she would kill them, and break the bones in their body.

She worked in my office every single day for the last three years of her life, worked in my campaign, got a lot of people off welfare, got honored by the House of Representatives, The United States Senate, and by President Bush. He wrote a letter praising her. And the Gannett Newspaper said she's a "suburban hero". She was really a remarkable person. She made a difference in people's lives. So I was very proud of that.

I also set up a committee, the "Have a Heart For The Homeless Committee," that provides loans to homeless, or near homeless families, and we've helped over 150 families. I raise the funds on my own. We have some student dances and some foundations and things like that. It's not a major thing, but people come up to me saying there's a problem and they'd go through the government and couldn't cut through the red tape, so I would do it on my own.

There's one woman for example, that caused me to form this. She was 76 years old and they were going to evict her from her house because the landlord wanted to raise the rent by $225. a month. I said I'd drive her to court and I felt sorry for her and I said to the judge, "Ok, I'll pay it--for life." And he said, O.K., so I signed a stipulation. Then I said, this is really stupid. So then I formed "Have a Heart For The Homeless" and we paid, and I think she lived about 18 months. Then there's a woman about a year ago who had a double mastectomy, was dying of cancer and we paid over $200. a month toward her rent until she passed away.

We helped one man which I was very pleased with. A carpenter fell down a flight of steps, he became disabled. He was living in a car with his son and wife. We found him an apartment and paid $1200. towards the rent and the security. Not only did he pay it back but gave us $500 on top of the $1200! So I thought that was interesting.

Westchester has about the same percent of homeless as New York City. The agencies now report people to me 'cause we have six or seven thousand dollars at any given time. So today, I helped one person and yesterday, I helped one person, or I could go two weeks without helping anybody. I used to help like one person at a time and do the whole thing. Now I'll give $150. or $200. towards the rent and do it with about 5 other groups screening the same person. And we're asking more people we help to do volunteer work for not-for-profit groups before we help. We try doing little things to get them out of their cycle of dependency.

I get a sense of satisfaction, like yesterday, people at one of the meetings were complaining about a roadside where it's very slippery and cars can fall into a ditch. So we put drainage pipes under the ground, and now it's going to be level. I was excited. Now I don't think there's many people who would be real excited about a sidewalk repair, a road repair job, but I felt comfort, you know. To me it is a great feeling that I got something done. A couple months ago, people complained to me. They said that the old sidewalk in North Elmsford hadn't been fixed in about 20 years. They complain, and complain, and nothing ever gets done. So I called the commissioner and said I'll do it myself. So that's when I worked on sidewalk repair and I felt here I did something. This job is really great because I announce that I'm doing something, and it gets done. Most other jobs as a legislator, you talk and talk and talk and maybe get one or two things done. Here, it's dozens of things.

Since I started my career, I've been sort of an outsider in the system. In politics you're always picked on, but I've been taking more of a maverick route so the political establishment hasn't really been pleased, so at times, people have been undermining or undercutting me. For example, I get annoyed with the newspapers sometimes because I don't feel that they're as fair as they should be. If there's one negative article or two, you take it but if you get it repeatedly, that's something that will upset you, but you can't let it go to your head. You just get aggravated and then a week later, a day later, you go back and do what you'd normally do.

People are generally positive and I've been pretty successful, though I've lost in a rush into the State Senate four years ago. It was such a big district and it's hard when you're running. I mean my style is one on one government and I really know a large number of people in the district, but when you're running in Yonkers or in a quarter million people district, it takes a long time to get known. I was running against somebody who is a familiar name, who everybody knew, everybody went to school with. I thought I was going to win because I had just won as County Legislator and won the vote with 70% and in politics your views are colored.

People say you're great and you start to believe you could be president in just a matter of a couple years. I ran and I knocked on doors. I got a very cold response. I didn't listen, you know. I'd go into a room and everybody's head was looking on the floor. They didn't want to talk to me.

In 1983, I was making about $20,000. a year, then last year ended with about $34,000. This year, it's a lot, it's $87,500. I take maybe one vacation a year. This year is not an election year so I'm taking one tomorrow for just a few days. I'm going to Cape Cod on a bike trip and I'm going for a week to the Grand Canyon on a bike trip. I did one camp trip two years ago in Iowa across the state. With

20,000 people, we biked from one end of Iowa to the other. That's a great trip. It was about 80 to 100 miles a day for a week. They took a college and the High Schools and just made tent cities all over. That was great.

Basically my problem is that I tell people what I honestly think and I'm not good at keeping secrets. I don't believe in lying or keeping things from the public. I feel that you might as well tell people what's honestly going on. I get sort of offended if I feel that other people are really taking advantage of the government, misusing a public trust. At the beginning of my career, I took away a lot of the town cars. The people were driving on vacations with government cars; I thought it was a misuse, so I stopped that. We had an auction for 15 cars. Also, I don't like it when the developers flaunt their influence and in the past, they seemed to get anything they wanted.

I've gotten some threatening attacks. My car was broken into in January. There were 6 town cars vandalized the second week in my job after I announced the car policy. Once someone called in the middle of the night saying "I'm going to kill you." A concession I got is a cellular phone that I leave in my car now. I voted for a group home for the retarded about 3 weeks ago and I was the only Council member who did and about 200 people or so, booed me. They were all angry that I did that. When it comes to property values, people get like crazy. Then I took some of the people on a tour of all the existing group homes in the town and they found out that they don't really have a problem. Though they disagree with me, I think now they just feel that I'm misguided, and they don't hate me personally. When I voted for West Top, the homeless shelter in Greenburgh a couple of years ago, I had gotten a lot of threats but people now are pretty calm and are friendly. I was bicycling there on Saturday and people were waving to me and chatting. People and politics have short memories.

It's a very interesting profession because I could do something for you, like let's say I help you with a Social Security problem today. Next month, there could be a problem concerning your neighborhood and if I can't solve it, you'll hate me. There's one couple, I introduced them. They got married on account of me and they moved to the district and then they had the homeless shelter right next to them, and then they hated me. I was the one who got them married, so it's strange. I'm still not married--but looking.

Politics is a strange thing. Now what I'm finding is when I'm joking, it gets in the papers. The newspapers take every word you say seriously. A newspaper reporter said, "What do you think should happen if the state legislature doesn't pass the budget on time?" I said that they should get the death penalty. This is a true story and the Reporter Dispatch put my picture in the paper and they had like three columns, one from the head of the business community, one from the Mayor of Elmsford and then me saying, "They should get the death penalty." I guess people don't understand my humor because I speak in a monotone and I'm not somebody who people think would be the life of the party, so, they took it really seriously.

When I took the people who were against the group home for the retarded on a tour a few weeks ago, I said, "I've biked every year to Vermont to raise money for the retarded, so maybe I should have abstained rather than voted for this." What I meant was that I was so committed to the retarded that I couldn't see myself voting against the home, and I could have abstained because I'm not going to be objective. So somebody writes a letter saying, "Even he says he should have abstained." So, you know, people take everything out of context.

I do very well with conservatives as well as liberals. I'm more liberal than conservative, but when people see me in back of a card table, and I help their parents get Medicaid or get a tax refund, they feel that I represent them. They're seeing me a certain way. Let's say I'm pro-choice, and they're a devout Catholic who's "right to life" all the way. They figure, how could somebody who's helping me be "pro choice"? They see you as the maker of day and light and then when you cast a vote, they say, "What!? This is the person who helps people!?

I feel someone wanting to get into politics should take an issue and work on it and get the satisfaction of making a difference, because one person can make a difference. You don't have to be a legislator, you don't have to be a mayor, you don't have to be a supervisor or a Congress person to have something you believe in, whether it's Amnesty International or whether it's a pot hole in the street.

I taught a course last semester on government in Mercy College and I required all the students to complain to the government. And if they got the complaint solved, then they didn't have to take the final exam. I find that politics isn't reading the theory books, it's really experiencing it. I think that there's nothing more rewarding than feeling that you can make a difference and I think that everybody could make a mark on society if they try.

What I have found is that if you're interested in a cause, whether it's the budget or getting a pool built or getting a youth center, it's really possible to make your voice heard. And that I think is the most important thing. The polls say that a high percent of the American people are dissatisfied with government so, the people who are dissatisfied should do something about it. Find one thing that you're dissatisfied with your local or county or state government and take action. Organize your friends, petition, write letters, get the newspapers to write editorials supporting your position. Maybe instead of being dissatisfied, you'll make a change. It might be a little change, but you could improve things and it's really not fair to always complain when you're not a partner because you really should be a partner of the process. If you don't like things that are going on, don't sit back and wait for the other person to do it--do it yourself.

I try my best by listening to the public and if I feel strongly about something, it's nice to feel I'm going to do something about it. That's why I like this job. I figure is it worth getting elected and reelected when you don't believe in what you're doing? And I made up my mind, I'm going to do what I honestly believe in and leave the chips fall where they will. Let the public develop their ideas and suggestions. I find people are really reasonable--that's the interesting thing.

Peter
Music Instrument Repair/Performer

When I was young, I imagined failure because of my family life, and in academia I was not successful--low grades. "Peter, what's the matter with you? You failed all the subjects. Idiot"--family, teachers. I started to blossom a little bit in late high school. I started to flourish. I applied myself and did well. I was not expected to survive my first year in college and I had trouble getting into college. I didn't know what to expect in the future. It was a matter of survival year to year.

Peter is one of a small and dying breed: independent professional music instrument repair person who is experienced, knowledgeable, and in Peter's case, a performer as well. An expert at repair and a virtuoso of many mostly wind instruments.

I never dared to dream of success, although when I started to repair, I dreamed that I would have a shop someplace in the basement of a house, and that people would come to me. I could see this as a happy way to live, not a high profile existence, meaning being a music teacher. I tried that. I don't think it was for me. I was a good private teacher; I could relate. I could talk to students, but I'm not drawn to being in the public eye or to be in front of a classroom. I was too insecure. The existence at a bench someplace where I could focus on something in my hands was much more appealing to me. I didn't want glamour. I wanted a happy survival on my own terms. That's what I hope for.

I repair musical instruments, not every instrument, mostly woodwind, brass and also violins and I call my instrument business "Orchestral Instrument Repair" which means instruments of the orchestra and that does not include guitar. I've worked in music stores and the guitar scene and there's no market for it. The market for guitar repair is cutthroat. There are so many people who do it and there are so many people who play, that it's unappealing to me, whereas wind instruments always was me, winds and violins.

I've played in orchestras, I've known violins, I've known violinists, I feel close to violins and I love the aesthetic of a violin, even though I don't play. I don't go all the way with violins. I can't make a violin play better. I can't buy a medium priced instrument and work on it and make it a high priced instrument. I do instruments for schools--cracks, bows, bridges, broken neck, refinish. That's basic carpentry. I don't make instruments. I can match up finishes, probably poorly, but it's enough in some cases. It's a nice break to work on something other than saxophone.

I could fix anything at this point. I know the process of learning, but one cannot do everything. You have to limit yourself if you want to be good. To attract a professional musician and his instrument, one needs a high degree of specialty, reputation, and through someone else they'll come to you. Do one person's instrument and that guy says "Hey that guy is good, take your instrument to him." The only thing I'll approach on my own are the schools, and colleges. I could even advertise to them, but I haven't.

I'm almost half way to where I want to be. I've been doing this for almost 18 years and I feel that my work is getting better. I feel that I'm attracting more of a quality musician whereas I've had trouble attracting professionals in the past. As one of my customers put it, he's really happy having found me, and he said that no one knows who I am, no one being the New York City scene, the guys playing the pits, in the studios. But I feel that I'm reaching out to them, that my work is reaching out, and I feel that's the only way you can attract people.

I have peak seasons, the summer being the peak. I've been working for the past six or seven weeks, seven days a week, anywhere from 5 to maybe 9 hours a day. When it's not busy, I work about 30 hours a week. It's enough for me. When you work for yourself, you don't think about the amount of hours, it's what has to be done. I don't think of it in terms of time. It's not like punching in and out. I've worked for retail outlets and when you punch out for lunch, and you punch back in, you get bawled out if it's ten minutes after the hour.

You go to work for a major music establishment, you see a lot of volume, you get a lot of experience and gradually as your reputation and skill gain, you break away from that store. The best way to leave is gradually. Now with Sam Ashe, I had to leave totally. I was laid off, because they decided that the music educational department was dispensable. The money was not worth it. We had a two-man repair shop, and they decided to cut it down to one person. The large corporations have a certain budget and certain money that they have to make and they're so large, that they cannot afford to delve into small markets which creates room for the little guy to get started. I've seen this happen with instrument makers. Of course, the big companies can sell more, but there are little guys that can make maybe three instruments a year. I'm thinking of early instruments because the large companies don't manufacture historical instruments. So there's room for the little guy to sell three or four a year and make a living, whereas a company will look at three or four a year and laugh and say, "It's not worth it, it's not worth the investment." Also, some companies can't afford to do repairs. It's cheaper for them to throw it out. Even if it's very repairable, it's not cost effective to pay somebody to do it. Throw it out, make another one. I'm no Mr. Corporation but I do know that people throw away stuff because they cannot afford to fix it.

However, the best way to go into business for yourself is to work for the large corporation. You meet people left and right, and they get to know you. You leave the store and give them a call. "Hey! Guess what? I'm on my own." "Oh great! I'll send you all my stuff!" That's how you get started, and if you're smart, you'll know you know next to nothing. That's right, if you want to ruin your reputation, start hanging your own shingle when you're real young and new at it. It's like painting a picture. You go to art school, are you an accomplished artist when you graduate? It's a trade knack to learn how to do it. Five years from that point, you're still making it better and you're still making mistakes. It's a very fine knack and it has to do with touch and feel. I do believe that if you want to have a long term reputation, don't blow it early. I look back at my work ten years ago, and I'm glad that I didn't really expose myself, because I know that I'm that much better now, and I'm still learning.

To be respected by a player, you must do consistently good work. The thing is there are a lot of schlock music repairmen out there. I hear that a lot and I see new work now from areas that I've never seen work from and it is terrible. I can see the older work on the instruments. It's just not right, and schools are paying top dollars, and they're getting schlock work because the large corporations cannot afford people of quality.

My situation is very good because people and the dealers bring me stuff and they pick it up and they say, "Charge me whatever you want" and I can get away with it, because the work is quality. If you can do consistently quality work, you can charge for it. I've been approached by someone who appreciates that and who's starting a business built on quality and he's been successful. His prices are high, but he's delivering. You might call me an independent contractor. I'm the repair department of his business, and I don't care, because I can charge retail. He comes to me, picks up and delivers. Instruments also come to me directly from schools, my own accounts, locally and also people who I've met over the years. They come to me from teachers who teach privately, the so-called off-the-street customer, plus I get professionals.

The repair school I went to was in the back of a large instrument company in New Jersey. It was called the Dorn and Kershner Instrument Company, run by three brothers and they were in the music business since the twenties. It was a multi-million dollar operation with a big building. And in the back, one of the brothers specialized in repair and he decided that he was going to have a repair school, The Eastern School of Musical Instrument Repair. It does not exist anymore; all the brothers have died. But it was the only repair school other than one in Elkhart, Indiana where all the major music companies are located. The only other ones I know of now are connected with degree programs in colleges. One could take a Bachelor of Music Degree program and you would be required to take the one or two semesters course in repair. Those schools have claimed that they are a repair school but the fact is you learn a bare minimum to function, maybe as a music teacher or as someone who can handle an emergency repair. I've known people who have gone to them and they've come out...well I could say that about the school that I went to; I came out and I knew very little. You really have no choice other than apprenticing.

Apprenticing is the best, but it's difficult to find someone who'll take you on because of all the problems with apprenticing. You know, you learn a little bit and you quit and go hang your own sign down the street. You're competition. "I studied with so-and-so," there's my reputation. So nobody wants to share the secrets. You find that a lot with violin technicians. It's very coveted information, more so than woodwind, it's weird. It's very difficult to find an apprenticeship for violins. The school had a string repairman there and on my breaks I used to go talk to the guy and he said, "Why don't you come in on Saturdays?" The school was five days a week, Monday through Friday. I came in and watched. I learned enough to get started and then, I'm just self-taught. You can't learn from a book. You can, but any trade, they'll laugh at a book. I've looked at all kinds of repair books, they show you something, they generalize and they leave a lot of stuff out. They leave what you need to know out. There's no step-by-step description.

Why it occurred to me to get into instrument repair, was my father was a tinkerer. He remodeled his house and all those years, holding a light for him. You know, I saw him using tools and the message when you watch your father do things is that things are possible and there's not such a big secret, veiled in some kind of hysteria. You watch him, and the tools were no mystery. I never saw him sick a day. He never took a day off. I never remember him saying, "I'm not going to work today because I'm sick." Never, till the day he died, and then he just died. When he died, that was it. He didn't suffer. There was no deterioration. It means that there is a work ethic, and I've been instilled with it. Work agrees with me. It's O.K. to work. Later on in life, I redefined the saying, that work <u>is</u> life. I read certain books like Walden Pond and learned that it's not whether you win or lose, it's how you play the game. It's not whether you're successful or how good you are that counts, it's process. The process of learning is the beauty in life. So when I thought of going into repair, it wasn't kind of a foreign, obtuse thought.

My uncle was a jeweler and I only met him like 5 times, but what I remember about him was that he worked at a bench and did close, fine work and he liked to make models of ships. I'd look at his ships and say, "Wow, that's really nice!" I was like twelve years old and I started building those clipper ships. I was able to sit for hours at a bench and make these models and play records. That was one of my favorite pastimes. That was the kind of temperament I had.

When I got out of school, I was faced with a big crisis, and that was I couldn't play. Everything that I had worked for up to that point fell apart on me. I just couldn't play. It was a breakdown. As my wife put it, my mouth fell apart. I had to face up to what I was going to do and at that time, it didn't include being the professional player and didn't include even becoming a teacher because I didn't think I could. I had planned to go to graduate school and get a teaching degree which I wasn't thrilled about, but I think the security-minded family upbringing told me to do something.

You can't just freeload. You have to plan. That was the message from my family, my father. I think my experiences said that the more planning you do, the more comfortable you'll be. You won't find yourself with some job that you really don't care about. Decide, be involved with the decision and be practical too, "Feed yourself, I'm not going to support you." He made that painfully clear. "I sent you to college, what more do you want?" It's then I decided to go to repair school.

So the crisis hit and I needed to know what I was going to do other than play music. I was riding in a car with a guy to a gig and he told me about a repair school, but I wanted to perform and my parents said, "Yeah, but what are you going to do for real? Are you going to play in smoke-filled rooms all your life?" In their opinion, there was nothing artistic about playing a musical instrument. It was all pretty "low class" stuff. They didn't appreciate what I was trying to do. And neither did I for the most part, at that stage. All I knew is that that's what I like to do. And all this talk about becoming a dentist, because I had two uncles who were dentists or being a lawyer or doctor, or something respectable didn't appeal to me. I decided, and it wasn't an easy decision, to pursue what I wanted to do.

I'm a conservatory trained musician. I did the whole thing. You get the complete picture when you go to the conservatory. I played jazz. If you're going to be a music store repairman, it's not necessary to do the conservatory. If you're going to repair instruments for the New York Philharmonic guys, yes, because you have to appreciate where they're coming from. You have to appreciate the instruments and the high degree of proficiency that an oboe or flute has to play at.

It is possible to learn how to play an instrument by taking private lessons; it's very ambitious. If you've ever tried to play an instrument from scratch you're lost, basically. But if you know another instrument really well, and you know the rudiments of music, picking up another instrument is less of a leap. I played recorder when I was in school and a clarinet is just like a recorder. It has stuff just like clutches, and side keys. It is a very understandable instrument. If one has no musical background, to pick up a clarinet is like learning Greek. It's difficult, but it can be done. You don't need the degree, but you do have to know where to put your fingers and what a clarinet feels like. And that's why this whole trade is a never ending scene. For me to learn what a professional knows, who has been playing his instrument for twenty years, to know what he wants his instrument to feel like, is quite an undertaking and the better I can do that, the more success I will have in repairing an instrument for that professional. That's my creed.

My father was not only handy but he also sang. When company would come over, my sister would play the piano and he would sing. He had his tunes, sort of pop/classical, semi-classical tunes and he was not embarrassing. He was really good. And a friend would come over with his family, pull out his trombone, sister would play the piano and I would sit and listen. I was the youngest of the family, with all the problems that go along with that like inadequacies, but when I started playing in sixth grade and they said, "Go ahead, you can play an instrument," I knew I wanted to try. And when I started to play, I just loved it. My mother never had to tell me to practice. I closed the door and that was it.

What I would recommend if you have trouble finding a musical scene to participate in, is to call your local community choir or a church choir. Even if you don't belong to the church, it doesn't mean you can't sing in the choir, providing you have certain skills. Go there and sing! Singing is great therapy. It's physical, it's musical, artistic--it's great! Open your mouth, use your body, it's like yoga. Get started that way. I've been fortunate. I have a lot of musicianship to back up my little vocal experience. When I got started, people said, "Come sing in this choir," and I got jobs right away, 'cause I could sing the pitches and the rhythm right the first time. I could sight sing.

I can't think of anything else I'd like to do. I'd like to work less, have less volume, more quality. That's why I'd consider training someone. Volume is death. Anybody who tells you something else is crazy. I'd like to have somebody from the New York Philharmonic trip up from New York just to come see me. It's a dream, and also I'm starting to think of having people work for me. But I don't want to do tubas!

I'm having fun doing this. I don't worry about success; the fun is getting there. So, if I fail, who cares! I'm still having fun. I'm the same as the next guy for suffering through a tough job, but the fact that I'm having a hard time is the beauty part of this trade. If it were all the same all the time, there would be no room for growth. So I don't worry about failure or success. I haven't had to deal with a success problem yet. I always read about people with lots of money who are doing drugs because they're not fulfilled. They're surrounded by things, everything they want and then they go nuts when they have everything that they want. Like Thoreau said, "Beware when you become accomplished, because that's when the trouble starts."

Into It

In order to find out what this business is like, you could be a clerk in a music store. You'll see salesmen at work, people who come into the store to sell their products to the owner of the store. You'll see teachers, the frustrations that they have. You'll see the music <u>business</u>. Absolutely do everything that your musical inclinations require you to do. I say require, because if you don't feel compelled to study music, you don't belong there. If you're doing it for some other reason, that's wrong. Just interested--thin ice! As a repair person I saw all the bullshit that was in music stores right away and I realized that I was in the best possible world. In the music business, the repairman is in the best place.

If you are sincere about your feelings in art, you can't lose. It can't be wrong. It's only wrong in the sense that you're in the gutter and you're a frustrated artist and have nowhere to sleep. My advice for finding a career is listen to yourself. Look inside. There's something there that you didn't know about, that you forgot about when you were ten years old. You liked to make models or something like that. I didn't know that was a skill or that was an "aptitude" till later. Don't discount things. Always try to be aware of something about yourself that you never noticed before. Keep pursuing quality no matter what it is, no matter what you do, whether it's digging ditches or doing auto body work, whatever. If you're pursuing quality and not pursuing the paycheck, that's the answer to success, psychological success. Pursue quality at all costs. Pursue doing that job, focus on that one little piece. Don't start saying, "Oh man, I don't have enough money; what am I going to do five years from now?"

I think the answer lies in the every second of existence. When you get frustrated, just look at the thing in front of you and concentrate on that, that's all. Make that the best paint job or thought that you're writing about. Make that the best thought you possibly can and don't worry about any kind of success or failure or anything else, just that one thing. It works when you're frustrated--"I wish I wasn't here; I wish I was doing something else." That's the time to really get disciplined. Slow down, because your body is speeding up. It's death. Slow down, one tiny thing at a time.

Tom
Accountant/Olympic Athlete

I think being street smart and book smart is probably one of the best things to be. My father didn't go to college, but he went to the college of hard knocks. Not that he learned the hard way, he just knows a lot, whether it's from reading or watching TV. Having a combination of both is probably the best thing to have. I think I learned from my folks and, I don't know if this sounds biased but, by growing up in the city and learning a few tricks. Maybe you learn quicker in an atmosphere where there's so many people and you almost have to, to survive. Not that I was allowed to do more, but I guess I do think I'm pretty worldly. At the same time I didn't have the best GPA in college, but I think that probably 60 or 70 per cent of learning in college is outside of the classroom anyway.

I asked the Olympic Committee for an Olympian to interview, but one who did not win a medal, and one who had a job to go back to. Tom is one of the most down-to-earth people I have ever met.
This interview took place in his Manhattan office.

I guess doing well in my grades and doing well athletically, people respect you more which is probably wrong. I was football captain and quarterback and what the hell's that? But because I was a leader in the school, I guess excelling in those two areas always made me comfortable. I always did well in math so I thought, let me try accounting. I knew it would be a pretty good job and neither of my parents went to college and I was like, this could be a good career.

I work for a public accounting firm. They do audits for public, as well as private companies. A public firm is one that's on the stock exchange. People invest based on an annual report and we sign that report with our reputation that says Joe Schmo has a million dollars in the bank. Our job is to call the bank and say, "Does Joe Schmo have a million dollars?" That's basically what we do, but there's thirty or forty different line items, like inventories. They say they own a building; we go look at the building. That's another test. And we audit and do tax preparation.

I'm working on a pretty important report regarding what makes up a successful person at this firm and we have a million different characteristics. The first thing we always look at is GPA, and why people get promoted. I've only been here five months so I'm like, what do I know? So we started off looking at GPA's, the schools they went to and SAT's which is basically high school. I think SAT's aren't so much what you learn from a book, I think it's a lot of experiences in life. It's from day one up to you're sixteen years old and how much you remembered. I think that kind of tells a lot about a person.

So, we're looking at what colleges these people went to, and based on the college, they think that might have something to do with how successful people are and I think that that's just absolutely ridiculous. A lot of people who are at the top level of management in this firm had very low GPA's. They had like 2.3's and I'm saying to myself, what the heck's going on here? It has nothing to do with that. It's personal communication, interview skills, things like that and you can't teach that. You either have that or you don't. It's kind of interesting, the report I'm doing. It's not like anything I studied in college, but I'm really kind of into it.

High School was weird. That's when we moved to Long Island. I think I was thirteen when we left Brooklyn and I was probably the most miserable person. I mean at that age, you have your friends, you have your little league, you have school and there's not much more in your life and that was all shaken up on me. I was pretty pissed off with my parents about that for awhile.

My father bought a house in a very nice area. It's just an hour from Brooklyn, fifty miles. It was in the summer which I guess is better than leaving midway through the school year and we moved to an area where there were a lot of kids my age. Instead of playing stickball, they played hard ball down at the park, so that wasn't much of an adjustment. School was school, except I didn't have to wear a uniform which I kind of liked. I got to wear jeans and sneakers instead of the tie and shoes. As tough as I thought it was going to be, it really wasn't at all. When I moved out here, the kids thought I was going to be a hood, 'cause I was from Brooklyn; they didn't know. They like, "Do you get into a lot of fights?" And I was like, "No!"

As big as Brooklyn is, it was very small for me. I mean school was a block away; we lived in an Irish Catholic and Italian area and it was the same at school. So I think my life was really small. And it was like, perfect. I had all my friends. I'd go to school and I'd play after I came home. I'd watch Star Trek or whatever, and we'd eat and I'd do my homework. I thought that was the way it was going to be forever. Then I found out there's more than three blocks away from my house. I guess I just figured it out when we left, when we were driving away. I was like, you're either going to mope around for a while, or you're going to make friends out here.

I have a sister who's a year older than me. I have a brother who is five years younger and another sister who's six years younger. Seemed like my older sister wanted to leave, I don't know why. And my little brother just didn't know any better. They thought we were going to my uncles for the weekend, or to the beach.

I thank my parents now. We always joke about it. It ended up probably being the best for me, athletically. I mean, there's no fields in Brooklyn. It's just millions of people and concrete. Now we have a nice yard and trees and it might be corny but the beach is five miles away, and there's just parks everywhere. We won the state basketball championship in my junior year in high school and that wouldn't have happened if I lived in Brooklyn probably. So as mad as I was when we left , I think it was great for me to leave, and I still have a lot of friends in Brooklyn. I meet them quite often. I have them for lunch up here a lot.

I guess I'm not the type of person, like a screamer. In high school before the football game started, the coach would call everybody in and one guy would stand there and then the guys would jump on top. I was never involved in that. I was quarterback and I always thought I had to be three minutes ahead of whatever was going to happen. I try to be low key I guess. I don't like the spotlight. I don't know if the word is conservative, but I didn't need anybody to scream in my face to get me ready for the game. I'm there; I know what to do. Get away from me, and I'll perform. I do think a team needs a person like a screamer. I think a team is made up of a lot of different types of people. Some people need it to light a fire under their ass, to wake them up for the game and I feel I'm here. Let's go. I'm going to knock you down, but I'll probably help you up or at the end of the game, I want to shake your hand-- probably not during the game, but I think that's the true symbol or the whole idea of competition. It's kicking somebody's ass for a half hour and then shaking his hand after.

Competition is mostly with myself. I'm on a team so I hope I'm not sounding selfish, but I always want to get better at what I'm doing. It's not beating the Soviet or Russian Team. If I improve everyday, that's pretty much what makes me feel that it is an accomplishment. Like every day is a stepping stone to getting better.

I play Team Handball on the U.S. Olympic Team and it's not handball at all. We call it Team Handball because there's a game in The United States called Handball, but the rest of the world calls Team Handball, Handball cause they don't have what we have, Chinese Handball or Four Wall Handball or Down at Coney Island Handball.

It's a big game in Europe that fifty years ago, they mainly played in the winter to keep the soccer players in shape. Visualize Water Polo without water; that's what Team Handball is. There's a goal at each end, and it's forty meters wide, and you dribble it like a basketball and instead of shooting into a hoop, you throw it into a goal. And there's a goalie standing there and he tries to not let you score. There's two thirty minute halves. It's not like tennis or racket ball or handball where a certain number wins; it's just like basketball, but instead of shooting, you're throwing.

You're supposed to lift up your legs, fly and throw the ball before you land and land on your shoulder or back or ass. And I always land on my feet and the coach is like, "You're doing it wrong!" and I'm like, but I just scored so be quiet! He says, "Don't worry, only the first one thousand times you do it, it hurts." You're running different plays and the object is to get as close as you can to the goal and shoot. So you try to distract your opponent with the ball over there, and then quickly bring it back when they're not ready, and different things like that. It's one point per goal and we usually say, under twenty goals, it's low scoring and if it's more than twenty five, it's high scoring.

It's very physical and the Eastern Block countries are the best. It's been an Olympic sport since 1972 for men and since 1976 for women and this was the first time the U.S. didn't qualify so I was pretty bummed out last summer after we didn't do it. Cuba was our qualifications, and we thought we had to win the gold to go to Barcelona, but it turned out that if we were to win only the Silver, we would have gone, because Cuba won the Gold and they didn't have enough money in their program to go. So the Silver Medalist went and it was Brazil. We got Bronze however. It was wild. Castro put the medal around my neck. I got a great picture of it. It was really unbelievable.

That's probably some of the best part, walking out on the field before the game starts, and the National Anthem goes off. That's when you think a lot like, what have I done to get here? I mean, I think back about a week before and then I think about a year before and then I think about...a crazy thing like I always think, if my grandfather didn't come over here, I wouldn't be here. There's just so many different variables that went a certain way, and that's why I'm here--like my father met my mother and my grandfather met my grandmother, things like that.

I think I get the competitive notion from my parents. My father's a very good athlete. He is probably more low key than me. The older I get, the more low key I think I get. When you're young and you excel at something, you want people to notice and the older I get, the more I don't care. As long as I know I get better every game, that's good enough for me. My mother's very competitive too; she's not as low key as my father. She likes to be in the spotlight. I think I'm a combination of both of them.

My father always did well; he played football and softball and it was fun. I always got to go to softball games and they did very well in all the different leagues in Brooklyn. He got to the point where he started coaching and was still good enough to play, but he didn't play. He let the other people play, and like I used to get mad every night, "Could you believe that? Come on!" I'm only eight or nine years old, so what the hell did I know? His teams always won 'cause he always had the right people in there and he always made the right decisions.

Most of my friends are good in math. We always watched sports and we didn't really read books and I think that got reflected in all our verbal grades, especially myself. I never read a book growing up, and now I'm on the train every night and I'm reading. I mean my mother's like proud that I'm reading "Mickey Mantle" or what have you. I'm into Tom Clancy now. I wish I read more when I was younger. It's kind of wacky, but the only thing I remember is Sports Illustrated and every day's newspaper.

We were in Czechoslovakia for 86 days in 1991 and I must have read twenty books. I read "War And Peace." My mother, in a letter she was writing me, was so proud. It's funny. I think everybody tells you to read "War And Peace" 'cause they're kind of pissed off after they've read it. I didn't think it was that interesting. Tolstoy and me,

I guess, aren't seeing eye to eye. I thought the history on the French Revolution and what was going on in Russia then was the best part of the book but the story on the side, I thought was slow. I read so many books over there.

When I think of my younger days, I always think of a team. I went from one season to the other, from football to basketball to baseball every year. I went to a small University, St. Bonaventure. Back in the seventies, they were one of the best basketball teams in the country and I went there in '85 to play baseball. I got cut from the team and I was like devastated because I felt I was good enough and the coach obviously didn't, and it was my second week in school and I'm away from my parents. I called my father right up and I was like, "Well, what do we do now?" You know, do I come home? Because I won't be doing anything. I couldn't not compete. I couldn't watch soap operas every afternoon after classes. I couldn't study all the time, 'cause I thought high school was more time academically than college was. There's only fifteen hours a week, whereas in high school you have seven a day, which comes out to be close to forty, or a little bit more than forty a week. And I could not do nothing. A lot of kids used to go party which I love doing too, but Friday and Saturday night was good enough for me. But Monday afternoon to Friday night I had to do something. I would have, who knows, I would have taken up archery or maybe even running, but that's probably where I realized that I was very competitive, that I just had to have something everyday. I could feel it, 'cause I wasn't doing anything for the first time in my life, and I guess I felt there was a loss in my life.

I happened to be fooling around in the gym and the basketball team had practice and they only had nine people and you need ten for a game. They asked me to play and I ended up making the basketball team which is the best team to be on at that school. So, things just worked out that I made the team.

I got a little burnt out from basketball. Division One is the only way I can explain it. Division One basketball is a business and it's not as much fun as it should be. I feel sorry for coaches, because their pay check relies on an eighteen year old kid throwing a ball through a hoop or ninety miles an hour in baseball. I knew I did not want to coach on any level like that. I've worked basketball camps and I would get more out of that than I would making fifty grand coaching college basketball. I recently got back working a camp in Cape Cod, and I had the young kids and it's just so rewarding; they're so much fun. They lose, they cry and I'm like, I almost start crying. I'm like, "Come here guys. Don't worry, we got another game tomorrow." So from that step, I knew I didn't want to coach.

What we have in The United States is called The Olympic Festival and what it is, is the Olympics of The United States. They break it up into four teams, East, West, North, South and based on where you live is what team you're on. We're the East. I had played handball in high school, city type of handball and it wasn't very organized. It was just like a million guys running around. It's like football in the gym. When it was raining, we played this. The reason we learned about handball is because it's an Empire State Game sport. And Empire State Games are basically the Olympics of New York .

The reason I got into handball at The Empire State Games is that tryouts for the team was at my high school. So we'd be fooling around up at the high school playing stickball or whatever, and they had Handball tryouts and we were like, "We could play this." We went in and since it's very similar to basketball--dribbling and running and jumping, and it's similar to baseball, we ended up doing well. It was five days up in Syracuse when I was like sixteen years old. It was like vacation, and it was a party. We were away from home, drinking. It was great! So, it was like an Olympic type of atmosphere on a very small level. So that's how I learned how to play handball. And we won a gold metal and we didn't know what we were doing.

The guys that played on Long Island used to meet every once in a while for parties and what have you. Then each year, the new kids would play and then some of us who had already played would go down and practice and teach them what we knew, which wasn't much because you don't play it everywhere.

When I came back from college, I hadn't played handball in like five years. But basketball is similar and I was in good shape and my brother started playing for Empire State Games and then I'd go down and see the old guys and I'm like, "How you doing?". We're older now and I'm working in the city meeting the same guys that you met five years ago who are on the corporate level now. So we started playing again.

It's kind of funny; the East Team is on Long Island because that's where the coach is from, so they had the team picked, except there was one spot left. A guy from the team calls me up and says,

"Can you go to the Olympic Festival?" And I'm like, "I just started my job," and he's like, "Can your brother go?" My brother just started a lifeguard job and he couldn't go so I said, I'll go into work tomorrow and if I can get vacation, I'll go.

It was two weeks in Oklahoma which was just a big party. It wasn't serious at all for me. It was a vacation, and I was going to act like I was on vacation, you know, beach, beers, broads. I was just twenty-three, I had already worked almost a year at the accounting firm and it's my vacation and I'm going away for two weeks to have fun first and play handball second.

I go to opening ceremonies and Ronald Reagan speaks. Bob Hope is there, Mickey Mantle, and I'm in Oklahoma. I'm saying to myself, "These people are serious!" They have The Olympic Oath; I started crying, 'cause I was thinking about the last twenty-two years of my life where I put almost as much time as most athletes here, but not for one sport. I'm saying to myself, maybe I should have, but it's all water under the bridge now. I'm twenty-three, I'm at opening ceremonies, I'm in tears. There's a kid, a crippled kid next to me. He's in a wheelchair and said something like "I feel sorry for the people who couldn't be here." And I'm looking at him and I'm saying to myself "You feel sorry and you're crippled." He was, I think, an archer or pistol shooter and he had like more gold medals than anybody. So I'm saying to myself, "What the heck have I been doing?" I'm not serious yet, but I'm saying to myself, "What the heck's going on here?" Then we have our competition and I wasn't playing much, because I didn't want to first of all, and they told me I wouldn't. But then a guy got hurt, so I went into the game and ended up being one of the leading scorers. The coach came after me, and he's like "We want you to pursue this and move out to Colorado." And I was like, I thought my athletic career was over, I have a good job.

In New York, you either go to Wall Street or you go to the MBA, basketball in college. And MBA would have been nice but I wasn't that good. The coach kept calling me up at my house after the Olympics. We got the gold medal, I don't know how. I'm saying to myself, no, this couldn't be happening. There was a trip to Germany, and Czechoslovakia coming up and I was like, I can't get off any more time, I just used it. "We want you to go, and we think you can be good." None of my family could believe it. My father said, "Do what you can do. You've never been to Germany; go!" So I went into work and I took a two month leave of absence.

I didn't know what I was doing in the beginning. This is the Nationals, preparing for the 1992 Olympics in 1989. We're going to play whoever will play us, pretty much, and it's no expense on my part. It's like training, slash experience. Most of the guys are already in shape 'cause they had already started training, but a lot of them went there after college. A lot of them didn't go to college and they moved out to Colorado. I went on this trip, I'm getting better everyday and they asked me to come up full time on the national team.

We played just about everyday for five weeks while on tour, so it wasn't sightseeing and it wasn't vacation, but it beats the hell out of work. I mean, Jesus! Everything's paid for and you're in places you would never be and I was like, this is pretty wild. But now my brain's going crazy. Like, you just got a great job, and there's six big accounting firms in the world and I was working for one. You're almost set for life, and they want me to throw this away and throw a ball around. I'm saying to myself, you're not even contemplating doing it. Then we worked something out that I move my job out to Colorado Springs, and the fact that no one knows about this game is not a problem to me 'cause I don't care. I'm doing it for myself and for the feeling I get out of it.

I go into my job like a knucklehead. How can I do this and always have something to fall back on? I took a one year leave of absence just in case it didn't work out, so I have something to fall back on. Everything turned my way and made it that much easier. Neighbors who were so excited for me, they're like, "You gotta go, you gotta go, you're only young once, bla, bla, bla." And I'm saying to myself, financially we're not poor, but I was making almost as much one year out of college as my father was making and I was kind of throwing that away. Not that I was supporting my parents, but I was contributing and I felt good doing it. They just did for me for the last twenty-two years and now I had the resources to buy a microwave every six months or stuff that my mother needs, things like that and I wouldn't be able to do that.

It's really weird. You live at the training center, you get free room and board. It's like going to college with no classes, but in place of classes is four or five hours a day of training. Looking back, if I didn't have the job to fall back on, I don't know what I would

have done. That would have been an unbelievable decision to make.
My hair would have fallen out. I was the only one in that type of
situation, so nobody could really tell me what to do or give me any
advice.

The first thing we did at the training center is go to the world
championships and we weren't involved, we went to watch at first.
All the best teams were there. Except for Cuba, I think our team has
the best athletes in the world. I was watching and we couldn't have
beat probably half the teams there. There are sixteen teams, but we
are better athletes than all of them.   Say my cousins, who are pretty
good athletes, play the Czechoslovakian National Basketball Team.
My cousins might beat them, because we're better basketball players,
it's one of the first things we did. But they're probably better,
athletically than my cousins. We run, jump and throw as good as
anybody in the world, but we lose to everybody 'cause we don't know
what we're doing.

So we went to play and I was like, all right, I'm serious, let's get
moving here. That trip was to Iceland, Luxembourg, Germany and
Czechoslovakia and then our next trip was to Korea and Japan.
These trips we do every six or seven weeks. In other parts of the
world, it would be the equivalent of playing St. Johns for a few games
and then going to play the Nicks, the Nicks being the national team,
and St. Johns being like a club team. When we first started out, all of
St. Johns killed us and all the Nicks really killed us. They taught us
lessons. But now we beat all the "St. Johns's" 'cause we're getting
better and the games against the "Nicks" are a lot closer. And that's
why I'm really into it now because we're getting better and as time
goes on, at Atlanta, hopefully, we'll be peaking then and anything can
happen.

I can sound like the biggest kid there is. I'm very sarcastic, I like
having a lot of fun. But at the same time, I guess I know when to be
serious--from 9 to 5 in this office. I try not to be a goofball or
anything like that but at a bar, I'll put gum on somebody's chair or
something like that. I live to have fun and being serious at the job. I
get enjoyment out of playing handball _and_ working.

My coach is kind of a character. We use a lot of different tricks
that we need to use to play at a level above us. It's all legal but it gets
you your edge. We do a lot of things where you could make mistakes,
like high risk plays. Like in football, there's one play that's hardly ever
run. The quarterback gets it, drops the ball, runs one way and the

guard will pick up the ball and run the other way and the whole defense goes with the quarterback. But if one guy doesn't get fooled, the play's a bust.

If you throw the handball like a baseball, it doesn't always go that good. If you throw it with backspin, it goes exactly where you want it to go. There's another shot where if I throw my elbow out, the ball will completely backspin and it will look like I'm throwing it fast, but it'll go super slow. That's my favorite shot. And the goalie, the first thing he does is blink. He thinks it's coming fast. He tries to cover as much of the goal as possible and if the first thing he does is blink, when he opens his eyes and the ball is still coming, it's funny.

If you're playing defense, and I have the ball, I'll just look like I'm going to throw it at your face and what's the first thing you do? You block and by the time you do that, I could be past you. We do a lot of different things like that, because we've got to almost cheat to stay at the level the rest of the world is at 'cause I've only been playing two years and the rest of the world's been playing as long as I've been playing basketball, say 20 years.

It's very appealing to the crowd. So wherever we go, we'll get killed by ten goals and they'll ask us for autographs. It's kind of funny. I think the fact that we're Americans is a part of it too. When you go to a country like Romania or Hungary, the people are there to see us also.

So I'm lifting weights now, and I'm running, and I'll probably play in a basketball league, a corporate league just to keep the fat off. In the meantime, I'll hopefully go on some trips with them and I'll be in shape. I'll make sure I stay in shape, aerobically as well as weight lifting. What happens if the guys start getting real good and I'm not there, and my standing goes down to say eighteen or nineteen and I want to be in the top sixteen 'cause that's who goes on all the trips? That's another decision that might have to be made. A lot of people are asking, "When are you going back?", which is ridiculous now I think, because it's a question I don't really have to answer since I'm not at the crossroads yet.

I want to not be known as a jock; I want to be known as an accountant right now, 'cause that's what I studied. I put playing on the back burner for a while. Who knows how much I would have learned in the last three years if I had worked steadily as an accountant? How business-wise would I be? Each day here, I get a little bit more responsibility and I'm getting my own projects. Right now, after my family, work is probably the most important thing I have going.

I have more of a problem getting up in front of twenty five people than I do 25,000. I don't know if that makes any sense. There's a difference between being nervous and having butterflies. Butterflies has something to do with wanting to play and part of the reaction is wanting. If I had the nerve, I would tell high school kids to study as much as they could. Don't waste much time, try to get the best grades you can and be in as many clubs as possible. And I think getting an A in calculus and getting an A in auto mechanics should be at the same level and it's probably not in most high schools. They don't take the auto mechanics as seriously as they do the calculus student and I think they should. I think the calculus student should take auto mechanics or wood shop, 'cause I think that helps you become worldly.

You're always going to have your friends at home, and you can hang with them on weekends and I think that's important, but they're not going to have the same group in the math class as in the auto mechanics class and I don't know if it's meeting the people or just working with them that makes you see. I think it's pretty important to just meet a lot of people and interact with them.

Handball is fun, but I don't want to lose. I want to knock the guy over in front of me, but after the game, I want to drink a beer with him. Not everybody can do that. A lot of guys on our team hate the other team and don't want to shake hands after and that kind of bothers me. But that's them. I don't know what it is, but there's a time to be serious and there's times when I can play on a girls' team, like I do at tennis camp. If somebody said to me there was a softball team here, "We want to come in first place, there's a certain amount of money and prestige and we want you to be part of it," then I'd play on that team but if at the same time, a girl came to me and said, "We're getting a team just for fun," I'd like that just as much. It's weird; I can do both.

If I'm playing with kids and somebody, say in volley ball, spikes the ball and tries to kill a girl, I'll be really pissed off but at the same time, if the ground rules are set first and we want to win and be serious, then I want to win and be serious. If we're playing fun tennis, say couples, unless we agree otherwise, then I'll just play for fun and I can have just as much fun doing that as I can kicking the shit out of somebody.

They always said you should always try to be good at one sport, all the coaches, growing up and the three big sports that I loved and played the most, I'm not doing any of them now. From the beginning, the one that they said I was the best at, I ended up not doing that well in and the one that I thought I wasn't the best at, I ended going the furthest in, meaning basketball. And now, of all three, the one I'm doing, I pretty much walked into by accident and this could take me the furthest--the Olympics. That's the furthest you can go in this sport. And the other sports, I didn't even get close to going to the furthest.

People thought I was crazy 'cause I liked accounting, "They're nerds and have no personality." But I did well and I liked it and I wanted to do it. I think accounting is good. An accountant can do marketing, but a lot of marketers can't do accounting work. I think it's pretty broad-based, accounting. You get your feet wet in a lot of different things.

Who'd ever guess I've been to Europe 6 times in the last year and a half. I've been to Asia, Cuba twice, Iceland, Seattle, the whole west coast and I thought my athletic career was over except for Sunday morning "fat man softball." It's weird because now I've got this new philosophy about sports, that eighteen year olds aren't ready for college, athletically, as well as mentally.

I don't think going into the army is a bad idea for a year or two, for kids to develop physically, 'cause I haven't even reached my athletic prime. They say Larry Byrd and Michael Jordan had their best years when they were twenty eight and I'll bet you there's people who might have been better and they stopped playing because maybe they didn't do well in college or for a million reasons. I think about that a lot. It's a shame for those people, that they didn't get a chance to excel because they weren't good between the ages of eighteen and twenty one. Carl Louis is thirty one years old and he's still the fastest person in the world. I'm twenty six and the average age on the team is twenty seven. In Europe, the average age is around thirty three so from that standpoint, Atlanta is going to be the perfect age for me. When I think about that, I'm like, don't fuck up--go!

It's funny, through word of mouth a lot of people know where I've been and they'll like--"I used to be great at handball, my father was the best down at Coney Island" or something like that. If I want to be disturbed or if I'm showing interest in this person, I'll say, "You have no idea what handball is." But if not, I'll say, "I'll bet your father was a good player!" And I'll just say, "See you later." Most of the time, I try to explain it, but it's a pain in the ass after awhile. Handball--It's not off the wall!

I don't know how everybody else's relationship is in my family, but I think mine is the best one of all of them. I'm closest with my oldest sister 'cause she's a year older. We did everything together, so I think I'm closest with her than with my brother and my younger sister. My brother, I would do _anything_ for him. I try to give him as much as I can from anything that I have. I don't know how to show the magnitude of love, how proud I am that he's my brother. My younger sister, I just think that she's a blast. I think we have a great relationship. She's kind of a goofball. She's not that book smart, but she's very street smart and we have a lot of fun together. It's kind of weird. I don't know how any of their relationships are, but I don't think anybody's is better than mine. I'd like to hear their views on that.

Jill
Jeweler/Trucker

I still fight with myself and have trouble working because if I'm having this much fun, how can I take my work seriously? The part of me that knows better says, "Isn't it wonderful that what you do is what you love?" And the other part's saying "If it doesn't hurt, it doesn't count." When people started buying my work, I'd look at them out of the corner of

my eye--you're really going to put this on your body?! I knew my mom would, but I didn't realize other people would. My father took ceramics and after one course he came away saying, "Now I can teach ceramics, because I'm one course ahead of the beginners--I could teach beginners!" I thought, if he can consider himself a potter after one course... I had been making jewelry since I was nine years old, majored in it through college and still didn't consider myself a jeweler or a silversmith, but just somebody who was playing. Recalling dad's attitude helps me snap out of it and take what I do a little more seriously.

I started taking classes at a workshop, when it was offered on Saturday mornings to children. I would take a jewelry class and then I would take a woodworking class, and I'd like jewelry better so I'd take another jewelry class, and then I'd try ceramics and I'd like jewelry better, so I'd take another jewelry class. My first projects were twisted wire bangle bracelets. They had the number one, the number two and a number three bracelet which had different combinations of wires in them and varied in their degrees of difficulty. I polished up what looked like just a piece of metal after I finished making the first bracelet, and the shine appeared. To my nine-year-old eyes, it looked like it came from Georg Jensen's! I gave it to my mother and she was thrilled. It was such an exciting thing for me as a kid to do something that looked so professional. With clay, there's not the same kind of intrinsic beauty to the material. If it's a bad looking pot, it's a bad looking pot when it's done. On the other hand, a bad looking piece of jewelry when it's polished can look pretty good. So I was hooked.

I continued taking jewelry classes and by the time I was a pre-teenager, the other students were asking me, when the teacher was busy, what to do because I knew. So my teachers said, "I think you're ready to go into the adult class, even though you're not an adult." That was a real ego trip to hear that I had become that good. So I attended the adult classes, and soon the beginning adults would ask me questions. It was just one wonderful experience after another, where I was not only thrilled with the process and the materials and working with my hands, but I was also getting this kind of feedback. The instructors and the director started to take me under their wing. I was becoming their protégé.

When it came time for college, I was applying to liberal arts schools, not really being enthusiastic about it, and not even getting accepted by half of them. I think the interviewers must have picked up on my apathy. My parents said "What is it you really want to do? What do you like to do?" And I said without thinking, "I like to make jewelry." I didn't take it seriously. It had always been my hobby. My folks' response shocked me, "Ok, you're going to make jewelry."

We went to one of my workshop instructors and asked him what the possibilities were for earning a living in the field of crafts. He was an old very wise master metalsmith who worked in spite of his Parkinson's. When he was soldering, he could keep his hands still for a moment when he had to apply the piece of solder. He said, "I predict that there's going to be a craft revival." He said, "People are going to be working less and have more free time and they will want to develop their interests." It was the early sixties and sure enough what he said did come to pass. Everybody was really hot for crafts and taking classes. So, that's how I got the courage to take it up as a profession.

I received a Bachelor of Fine Arts Degree from R.I.T.'s School for American Craftsmen with a major in metal work. Then I got most of my work done towards a teaching certificate and a Master's in Art Education. I didn't finish it. I was to do practice teaching and I was in Rochester, New York. I asked my college if I could do regular teaching instead of practice teaching. They said if I did six months in a recognized public school system instead of my two months of practice teaching I could get my teaching certificate and finish up my Master's by coming back and taking courses in whatever I wanted. So

I lived through a nightmare of teaching art in public school. I used to pray that the car would get hit by lightning on the way to school and put it out of commission, at least 'till three o'clock. I hated it.

When my obligation was over I wrote my college advisor and said I was ready to come back and get the rest of my credits and my certificate. He said, "We've changed our mind. We don't want to screw up the credibility of the program." It was newly recognized by New York State as an accredited program authorized to give the certificate without the students having to apply to the state. He said, "We don't want to make exceptions and take a chance that it will ruin us with the State. Come back and do your practice teaching." I didn't want to set foot in another classroom. I figured I'd never want to teach in public school again anyway so what did I need the credentials for? Sometimes I regret that I didn't fight it, but I had nothing in writing about our agreement.

So I just thought that I wasn't a teacher. And then I went to teach in the workshop at which I'd studied for so many years. People were there because they wanted to be: they weren't there because it was an easy credit or because they could talk to their friends during class, and those who were disruptive I could tell to leave. It was a whole other experience. It was a wonderful experience. I turned them on, they turned me on. I was a teacher. I could really communicate what I was doing and if somebody didn't get it, I could come in from another direction. I had the ability to reach people in ways that they seemed to really enjoy and to this day, people will come up to me in a shopping mall and say, "Are you teaching? You're such a wonderful teacher." It was and still is a great experience for me.

After college I bought a little industrial building. It had been a picture frame manufacturing business, and the man who owned it died and his widow was selling it. It was being used for storage when I bought it. It was all boarded up and the windows were all broken. It was really a mess and it had never been lived in. It had been built as the Portuguese American Social Club by the members of the club. There was a bar and grill downstairs and a dance floor upstairs. There was no plumbing or anything upstairs. It was just a big space.

It was so dilapidated, I had to put in a front door. It wasn't insulated or livable. It was an industrial green inside with greasy stuff all over the floor that I had to scrape up over a period of a year with a razor blade. I had a wonderful time doing it myself, shoving paper towels into the big gaping holes where the nails had held the wood latch that keep the door closed. I had to have a licensed plumber and a licensed electrician to get a Change of Use Permit and a Certificate of Occupancy. Once in a while, I had a carpenter help me as well as friends and my parents.

The downstairs area is my studio, and I taught in it for years when it was a wet basement. The first thing I did when I bought the building, was tear down a wall in the basement to see what made a building. I wanted to know what was behind the cheap wood paneling. I had never been able to do that either. I took down this wall, and looked at the stone foundation of the building which had some black waterproofing stuff on it. I could see at the top of it a little light coming in from outside.

I took sheet rock that I had been pulling down from upstairs and a little saw and I cut out leaves. I painted the sheet rock pieces green and fall leaf colors and put them at the top of the uprights, the "tree trunks." It was like being in the woods, in a comic book kind of way. I taught there but the problem was that it would get wet when it rained and I'd have to send my students home. Later, a local contractor laid the floor, put up the walls, built in the shelves and the closet, and it became a nice room. He cut open what used to be the men's room, and that became my work area.

I taught about 125 students a week during each term. I did that from about 1965. I started teaching in the summers assisting another instructor and alone while she was on vacation. In 1968, I started for real when I taught public school. It was kindergarten through twelfth grade art. Two schools had lost their art instructors, so they just put me in there. They were in a bind and needed somebody desperately, so they took me. I had done the work, but was not certified. I worked on an emergency certificate for six months.

I started entering craft fairs, and I would bring my work and stay for the week. I'd have to create a space to sell my work in. It was about 8 by 10 feet. I provided carpeting, back drop, tables, chairs, lights and cases. They'd have wholesale days on Tuesday and Wednesday. Thursday was a layover day and then the general public would come for the weekend. So there'd be wholesaling and retailing at most of them. Besides selling directly, I would take orders and fill them after the fair.

That added to my income. I'd usually have a student, an apprentice or my mother or friend work with me. It was exhausting, but I felt very fortunate to be a jeweler and be able to carry all of my work in an attaché case and watch the potters and the glass blowers come in with their newspapers and cartons. I never realized when I went into the field what an advantage that would be. And things didn't break very easily if I was reasonably careful.

I've been told that one can expect eventually, to get Carpal Tunnel Syndrome, working repetitively with pliers and that kind of thing. I don't know any jewelers who have been at it for a while, who don't wear glasses. I developed a sensitivity to metal. I have to paint the inside of the snaps on a shirt or jeans with nail polish or I will break out. I can't wear a watch or earrings or anything with nickel in it anymore. So I think that when you work with something for a long time, your body gets sensitive to it. I'm more aware about that now. I have better ventilation in my studio than ever before. Fumes that used to turn me on, turn me off now. We used to use asbestos to solder on, and now there are substitutes.

I entered only juried craft fairs because at flea markets, people want to haggle. They want to get a good deal--that's what they're out to do. But at a good craft fair, people come knowing the quality they can expect and they don't haggle. I did a local street fair, and sold one fifteen dollar ring. That's just not my market. My work is labor intensive so I can't sell it cheap. Some have their pieces manufactured in a country where the labor is very inexpensive, and they do and redo the same piece. They might change the stone that's in it, but its other components are virtually the same very often. Or they're working very quickly with little material. They're skimping somewhere where I'm not, either in the material or the quality of the workmanship, or the amount of money that's paid to the person who's doing it. When I went into production and I had molds made of my work, I could sell it for less. That fifteen dollar ring was a cast ring. It wasn't a one-of-a-kind piece. I'd rather teach than become a jewelry manufacturer, because when I become a jewelry manufacturer, I feel pretty far away from the creative side of the work. It's not so much hands-on. There are spurs to cut off from castings, filing, and polishing and that's it. It's not the same. If I'm teaching, I'm sharing something that I love to do with people who want to learn it, and it's stimulating to me. I help solve the problems they have with their work, so I'm doing some creative stretching myself. With the manufacturing, I have to be a better business person and job delegator and I don't enjoy that so much.

I think artists tend to be shy and to go out and sell themselves is hard. Some do it very well, and some people whose work is not all that great, do a lot better than I because they're good business people. Their pride in their work shows. They believe in it and they think a customer will love it. They have a wonderful attitude about it, and they can sell it to a gallery or to an individual comfortably. To sell my work, I bring it to a gallery and they take it on consignment, or buy wholesale. Sometimes I sell it at a private sale at my studio, or I'll participate in an exhibit and people see it and there's a price list with it.

I always wanted my work to sell itself. I wanted people to walk up to it, and love it and want to rip it off me. I wasn't comfortable talking somebody into one of my pieces. When I say something nice about my own work, I feel like I'm bragging. When I suggest somebody buy it, that it's perfect for them, I feel that it sounds insincere, even if I really believe it. It's just hard to do it because I think, coming from me, it's different than coming from another person. And I've been sold things by people who've made them and been tickled to death to have interacted with the person who made it, so go figure! You hear it so often, it's trite, that whenever a person is making a piece of art, it comes from them so it's got to do with offering part of themselves and not wanting to have it refused.

Occasionally, I'd bring my work into a store and they'd say, "Why don't you put more colored stones on these pieces? My customers want colored stones this year." I'd have to put up with that kind of thing. I make a piece because of something that I'm expressing or feeling and somebody's telling me how to make it more marketable. There's something about that, that I don't enjoy. I'd rather teach than deal with that. I don't enjoy the process of selling-- the standing around and waiting while the gallery owner attends to his or her customers; waiting for them to look at my art and relate to it as merchandise. I'd rather somebody else did that. I should probably have a rep.

In addition to jewelry, I make small metal sculpture and other small objects. I do little functional things like hors d'oeuvres sets, cigarette lighter cases, bells, candle snuffers. Silversmithing techniques may or may not be used or I might build it more like a piece of jewelry. I made a complex piece for my thesis, a chess set, and the reason was because it was the only time in my life I could spend thirty-five hours a week for eight weeks on one piece. And, I wanted a handmade chess set. It was a great opportunity to express myself, philosophically. To relax, I usually do something else, like make greeting cards, note cards, gift wrap, or I'll beachcomb, scavenger hunt, take pictures, something totally different. I dabble.

I loved the world of the craft person. I loved dressing in jeans when it was, and wasn't fashionable. Artists could get away with murder that way. They could have their own spirit and people would just say, "Oh well, they're artists." I liked not being bound as so many of my friends were. My instructor at R.I.T. was a Dane, and the Danish-modern influence was strong for me because of him. He learned in the apprentice system and it was eight years before he was allowed to work in silver. It was an old traditional system.

The process is more like inventing the solutions. So that's the creative part, being clever, resourceful, designing something that feels right, looks right, works together. Sometimes, I'll turn the piece around and see if I can get a handle on it from another position until I either don't want to do it anymore because it's not going any place special to me, or until everything is done. It's a feeling. If I go too far, or it's just not right, it may become the scrap from which a piece will start a year from now. I'll cut it apart, or I'll rework it. Eventually, I may use it to do what's called charcoal casting, where I'll carve a design into a charcoal block, and I'll melt the thing on top of the block and I'll press it with another block into my carving. Or I may fuse pieces of it together and create a kind of collage. If none of the above comes out to be satisfactory, I sell it back to the company from which I bought it as scrap and I buy new material. Silver has intrinsic value which is another wonderful thing about it. It's not a total waste, even if the piece is a waste.

Gary, my husband, drove into town in his big tractor trailer. I had met his brother in Nebraska the year before on an automobile trip I had taken. He was a trucker. He went to work for Gary and when they came East, they stopped by to visit me. That's how I met Gary. I had been writing to Gary's brother, because when I met him I spent a day with him in his truck making deliveries through three states unloading steel off the back of his flat bed, in the rain. I was so excited by being up in that big truck and driving down the road with the windshield wipers going in the middle of the night, and dropping off this steel in the mud. The whole thing had a mystique to it that just appealed to me. I said, "You know, I'd really like to do this, because my work always kept me in one place, my studio." I wrote him and said, "I need for you to keep in touch with me, to keep me motivated here, because I'd really love to do that." When I met Gary, he was hauling furniture for an agent of United Van Lines. Three months later I flew out to Denver and hooked up with Gary and his brother and learned to drive the truck. I really didn't have a job anymore when my summer classes ended.

I got started driving by sliding into the seat behind the driver and he would get out of the seat going down a straight flat road at about sixty miles an hour in the middle of the country. The truck had eighteen wheels and thirteen gears, which I didn't know how to shift for three months, so I only drove as long as it was on the flat dry highway. Gradually I learned to shift and to go into the truck stops and pull into a parking space. I got a permit from New York and a license in Arizona where I didn't have to test on a truck. I could take the written drivers' test about a truck, but I could take the driving part of the test in a car. I figured a license, even if it's not from my state, is better than no license at all. And then I got certified by United Van Lines as a second driver. I had to pass a driving test with them, about an hour long through downtown St. Louis on a holiday weekend. It was really scary going through construction, rural areas, and city areas. I made it. I started filling out logs, because I was now required to and when I had a year or two of log books, I went to the New York State Department of Motor Vehicles and showed them that I'd been driving. With a 90% on my New York written test and with my log books, they licensed me. So finally I was completely legal, with a New York State Class 1 driver's license.

When Gary and his brother came to visit me, they were to be here through the weekend. They thought they'd pick up a load and go somewhere else, but the business was very slow at that time. They wound up staying fourteen days. I fell in love with Gary in the first three, and by the time the fourteen days were up, we wanted to be together. Then, when I was on the truck, we talked about getting married. I said I didn't want to be married to somebody who's not home at night, who's gone for weeks at a time. I said the only way I would do this, is if I could handle being out there too. So I had this tremendous motivation to make it out there as a trucker and I enjoyed it very much. I enjoyed seeing parts of the country I never would have seen otherwise, and a subculture I never would have known otherwise, and the life style which is hard, but poetic to me. The people I was meeting were unlike people I had ever been friends with before. I found it very difficult tolerating certain attitudes that people have away from the coasts, but eventually learned to be more accepting of a variety of opinions.

There were a lot of very capable women beginning to be out there driving. Some of them were forced into it, because it had been their husband's business, he died, and they had to continue to feed their family. And for a non-college graduate, it paid pretty well. That was before trucking was deregulated; people were making good money at it. I didn't look typical and as a matter of fact, as soon as we got away from the coast, before they would ask, "What's your name?", people would ask, "Where were you born?" "What's your nationality?" They just weren't used to seeing the likes of me out there. Most of them had blond hair and blue eyes. I don't. A lot of them were from the southern states or California. Not too many cross-country truckers choose to live in New York. There are so many beautiful and less expensive places in the country and they can live anywhere and be just as convenient to home.

One time we were on the border of Texas and Mexico and as long as we were parked there overnight, I wanted to go into Mexico and see what that was about. To go from the truck stop into a border town, we had to take a cab that was connected with a "house of ill repute" in Mexico. In order to pay the bill for the cab, we had to go into this place of business. It was a very unusual evening.

That was the interesting thing about trucking; every day was different. Every experience was new. The flowers were new, the bugs were new, the animals were new. I took a tool box with me. I thought I'd make jewelry when we stopped in between loads, but wherever we were, I wanted to see it. I didn't want to stay in the room or in the truck. We would sit in the truck and hookers would drive around on the hoods of the cars, bare-chested sometimes. People would hand out cards with colored photographs of different kinds of uppers and downers, and a phone number to call. They would deliver directly to the trucks. Some of it was pretty tacky-seedy, but I loved it.

I remember in Oklahoma being on the interstate in a wind and snow storm standing outside the truck with a flare and in a nylon jacket flagging the cars to go by, while Gary was under the truck with another flare trying to thaw out the fuel filter before the tow truck came to tow our big monster truck off the highway. Gary got it thawed just in time, and we pulled out just as the tow was getting to us. The weather, the fog, the ice storms down south where you wouldn't expect, all of it was exciting.

We had to go to John Hopkins to pick up part of a space satellite and had a courier come with us. He had to know where all the dry ice was along the way between Maryland and Florida, so that if this piece started to overheat, or the truck started to overheat, or a tire caught fire, he could keep the satellite at the right temperature. We also had a climate controlled van. The satellite was called an "Anti-Magnetic Particle Tracer Explorer" and we produced a third of it. Germany produced a third of it, and Great Britain produced a third of it, and we were all to gather with our parts in Cape Kennedy where they assembled it and sent it up. It sent particles into outer space where there was no gravitational pull, and then they traced where the particles went to see how different things pulled out there. The courier had spent two and a half years of his life on this one project and that's all he thought, dreamed, and talked about. He rode up in the cab with us. The first night we stopped, and the second night we drove through and we got in first! I drove in. I decided this is one step for womankind, and I drove into Kennedy! That was a trip, because there weren't that many female drivers out there yet, and the crew at Kennedy was noticeably startled. Truck stops by the way, are probably the only place where there's no line at the women's rest room.

The solitude of my work had already gotten to me when I met Gary. I was tired of being alone and hearing only my own voice or the supermarket clerks' voices during the day. I really felt, when I was trucking, that I was busting out of that. It felt wonderful. When we stopped trucking six years later and I started making jewelry again, I quickly became intolerant of the solitude again. At one point I was able to gather up some other instructors at The Workshop and say, "Let's come in sometime when the shop isn't being used and work on our own stuff together, just so we can talk to each other." I would do things like that, but basically I was alone. If I had somebody come in and work with me, when they were in my shop, I couldn't create. I could oversee what they were doing, but I couldn't create. I would look forward to them going so I could get back to being creative, and then they'd go and I'd get lonely. I thought that once I was married that would go away. When Gary was home every night, if I was home alone, ok, I'd have company later. But I'm still having a bit of a problem with it. His hours are long, so I'm still alone a pretty big chunk of time. I'll go into town to have lunch, just to be among people and that's about it on a good productive work day. Then Gary will come home tired, we'll have a little time together, and he'll have to go to bed. My natural time to work is from maybe one in the afternoon till three in the morning. So if I'm being true to myself, our hours don't even match.

Excluding the fact that there's a recession and that jewelry is a luxury item, I think it's a bad time to get into this business, unless you want to get into the <u>business</u>. But if you want to work in the style I've been choosing to work in, it's a bad time. It's something people don't need. There's a whole jewelry industry out there that one could get involved in, go to school for, and take courses and get certified in. There's bread and butter work like watch repairing and appraising. One can learn from reading, from watching other people work and by taking a course here and there. You can pick up a particular skill as you need it or want to use it. There are a lot of craft people in Santa Fe and California, for instance, but how viable it is as a way to make a living in some place like Nebraska, I don't know. It's best done in areas where there's a market for it, of course. So depending on what you're making, you could do manufacturing anywhere, the cheaper, the better. You could put your studio in a low rent district, and then do the craft shows and take orders, or become a manufacturer, and have sales people that take it to cities. I think there is always a market for classes too, for people who want to do it as a hobby, like at senior citizen centers. Jewelry making requires mostly small hand tools so it's not very expensive to get into initially. Rehabilitation programs could use it, camps could use it.

I have a "formula" for pricing. I calculate my materials cost, and I figure my labor at about twelve dollars an hour. I'd prefer it to be more like thirty, but that's ridiculous although that's what I can make teaching. Then I add about 10 per cent for overhead, forty per cent for markup (profit) and I come up with my wholesale price. Labor isn't profit. A lot of people confuse the two, but they're not the same. So I have come up with a price. I look at it, I laugh and then I think, ok, now what will it sell for? I investigate what is comparable to it out there in terms of quality and materials and so on, and I see where my break even point is before the markup. I see what I have to make just to cover my expenses. Somewhere in between there, and what I figured out my retail price should be, is what I price it at. It also has to do with how ready I am to part with the piece and what I think the traffic will bear.

Some of the prices just get so outrageous when they're one of a kind, because there's so much thinking that goes into it and so many hours. It may take a week to make a special complicated necklace. If I do it in gold, I can get paid for my time. If I do it in silver, I can't. People will pay more, because they feel like they're investing in the material. The labor can be absorbed more readily. It's a smaller percentage of the cost. With silver, the labor tends to be the bulk of the cost. I'm sure that with pieces made of platinum and diamonds it's relatively easy to get the price of the labor. If I do the same piece in copper, I can't get anything like what I get for it in silver although the labor is the same. The reason I don't use very expensive materials more often is that I don't want to lay out the money for the inventory. You're sitting with your money tied up and not earning anything until it sells. Also, I don't work as freely in something that's that expensive because I'm aware of everything I'm cutting off and every file stroke I'm making. The pieces tend to be much tighter, not as spontaneous. If somebody wants something in gold, I'll make it in silver first to work it out so I know exactly how much gold I have to buy and how to go about it. The gold piece becomes an interpretation of the original silver piece.

The chess set that I made for my thesis I had to write about and explain. I wrote what it represented for me. Years later in therapy I said, "You know, I feel like I cheated on my thesis, because I didn't think of what I wanted it to represent before I made the piece. I thought of it afterwards." And he said, "That's because your creation was in metal and your interpretation was in writing. If you had figured out what you wanted to do before you made the piece, the writing would have been the piece, the interpretation would have been the metal." When he said that, I realized, subconsciously I had put all that content in it. I just hadn't thought about it, but when I did, I saw what was there.

Lynn
Flight Instructor

I was invited to talk to a vocational training class, Travel and Tourism, and it was really kind of depressing 'cause all the girls in the class wanted to be flight attendants and all the guys wanted to be pilots! And there's nothing wrong with being a flight attendant, it's an important position, but it's just kind of depressing that they had never even considered, "Oh gee, maybe I could be a pilot, or maybe I could be a mechanic." The receptionist at my flight school is training in Power Flight Mechanics, a license to work on airplanes. I think that's really an interesting job. I'm fascinated by that now. I don't leave them alone when they pull apart an engine. It's kind of like math where there's a definite answer. There's a definite way in which the engine works together.

I didn't have a natural aptitude. When I started flying, I had no idea what an engine was. I do understand engines now, I learned. I think that it's just something that we've been discouraged from doing. It's just like math. I hated math growing up. I thought it was so hard and now I just think it's one of the only times in life when you get an answer! You get a positive answer, two plus two is four, and it always will be four and always was four. There are so many other things in life that you just don't get an answer to. It's very rewarding in that way.

The most exhilarating experience in teaching is that you'll have somebody who comes for a "Discovery Flight" where they do most of the flying. It's happened to me about four or five times, the person gets off and they just turn to me and say, "This has been my lifelong dream, and you made it come true and I can't believe I'm flying." You can see it in their faces, they're so excited, they're so happy. And I still have flights where I see things like a beautiful sunset and you know that nobody else has that perspective besides other people who are flying.

I'm not sure why Lynn agreed to being interviewed — she struck me as someone who had only one desire: to fly. I met her at Westchester County Airport and caught her in between flights.

Right now it is a bit easier for a female to get hired than it used to be, but I don't accept that it's reverse discrimination in any way because we're still such a small minority. Once you get there, you feel everybody assumes that you don't deserve to be there so you try to be twice as good as everybody else. I didn't find that to be true here but I think when I go on to get other jobs, if I go corporate or with the airlines, I'm definitely going to find it that way. You have to work really hard not to have a chip on your shoulder, because you're always competing.

Since I am in competition or in the ranks with a lot of men, it's hard in a relationship to back off on that competitiveness. I was out with a bunch of friends dancing and my friend threw up his arms and said, "I'm not dancing with you anymore 'cause you're leading." When I spend my whole day telling men how to fly and giving directions, it's hard in your personal life to back off from that. I Feel like I'm deflecting a lot of attention away from the fact that I'm female because many people think that you're using that for an advantage.

On the job, I have to dress like a male. You lose your female identity. Usually I have a pilot's shirt with epaulets and a tie on. That's pretty standard fare for any pilot anywhere. What you would think of as stereotypical female behavior is not acceptable, like reacting to stress and starting to cry. I don't think it's so much behavior that I have to change when I come in here, as just roles that we take on. You behave a certain way with your mother and a certain way with friends. It's not that much of a change in the flight school. Everybody is very supportive but it feels from my point of view that once I get into like a commuter airline, I'm going to have to take on a defensive role saying in effect, "Yes I deserve to be here."

Somewhere in college, I decided that I wasn't going to take anything for granted, that I was going to question everything. Not that I wasn't going to do what the normal people would do, not that everything that I'd been taught or that everything my parents did was wrong, but it's just that I wanted to know why! And I teach the same way. I've always been a strong believer that whatever you want to do, whatever you can control, if there's a way, then you can do it. I don't think that you should ever let someone say that you can't do something. My sister had a boyfriend once who said if you want either one of us to do something, forbid us to do it. That's really a good way to get me to do something--tell me that I can't do it.

When I was 17 I wanted to go into the Air Force and fly and my mother wouldn't sign the papers 'cause she wanted me to go to college. I thought about it but I think it was just rebellion, I don't think I really wanted to fly then. I had no idea what I wanted to do. I really would have been a great person to have a year off and do something and then go to college once I figured out what I wanted to do. I really wasted the first couple of years.

I learned a lot while I was in college but not that much from schooling. Looking back, I would have taken different courses and done different things. What I did was great for me, but it's not in terms of what I could have been doing for my career. College is the only time in your entire life that you can learn for learning's sake. You can take time to decide what you want to do. In high school, there are things you have to do. For all I did with my degree, it was learning for learning's sake. But it's nice to have a piece of paper at the end that says I have a college degree, I'm educated. But it might as well have been in philosophy. I got a degree in psychology with a minor in art. From a practical point it hasn't helped me.

I did an internship working for a photographer and he was off the wall. He kind of took me under his wing and he was a lot of fun. He used to bring me into the darkroom and tell me to scream as loud as I could just because he thought I'd never expressed that before or that I never had the courage to scream. And he always asked me things like, why are you doing this and why do you accept that? He got me thinking.

He just lived his life, not that it was so different but just his own way. And I had always cut my hair funny or had worn certain cloths to convey a message and he just <u>was</u> what he wanted to be instead of trying to prove to other people. He just was himself and take it or leave it. He definitely was trying to teach me that message. He got me questioning why people think that change, or something that is different is bad and his whole point of view was that something that's different, or change, is always a good thing. He started me thinking about that and how being black or Jewish or female is almost centered. There have always been things in my life that have somewhat set me apart. When I was younger, I really had a desire for everyone to say, "Here's Lynn, she's different, she's her own person."

I got a job as a photographer after college and it was great and we'd sit around at lunch and all the women would be talking about wallpaper and rug samples and I just knew that I didn't want to have anything to do with that. I wanted something else. I didn't want to go back to school. I was sick of school and I wanted to do something that was challenging.

I was talking about taking flying lessons for a long time and I put it off and off and then Christmas or my birthday, my boyfriend got me a "Discovery Flight" and then I just kept going. I think he was kind of calling my bluff, 'cause actually I was a little nervous about it too. The airport was near his house and I could see the planes and I would wonder if it would be fun. So he gave me a gift and my parents are still mad at him! That first time, the battery must have been dead because they had to hand prop the plane. The first three flights that I took actually, I can't believe that I sat there. I remember thinking, well the instructor's going up and so it must be O.K. but I was pretty nervous about it.

The great thing for me about flying is that it's almost like meditating 'cause you're concentrating so hard on what you're doing in the plane that everything else disappears from your head. It's like any physical skill that's really taking a lot of concentration. I find that pilots are very controlling. I'm a very controlling person and if I can control my whole world and control other people's lives, that's a real ego boost. You're completely in control. That's what most people are afraid of, people that don't like to fly. It's usually claustrophobia or that loss of control. It's like surgery. When you go on a flight, you're in that pilot's hands and you've never met that person before. I don't like sitting in the back of the plane and not having anything to do with it.

The first step toward becoming an instructor is to get your Private Pilot Certificate and you must have a minimum of 40 hours flight time logged. That allows you to fly with friends and family, not for hire. Then you get your Instrument Rating which allows you to go through cloud cover, then your Commercial Certificate which allows you to do some minor things for hire like banner towing and pipeline inspection, local sightseeing and instructing. You have to have 250 hours to get your commercial. You have to know everything well enough to teach it. You have to know about physics, weather, aerodynamics, you have to know how the engine works, flight physiology. There's a lot of knowledge thrown at you and it's really kind of overwhelming when you're studying for it and I'm really hard on myself.

My Instructor Rating Test was awful. As I was preparing for my test, the head of the school and other instructors were saying "Come on, just take it, you're ready, you're more than ready, you're over prepared". My examiner was...shorter than I am and he was a real bastard. He had an ego the size of Brooklyn. Most people have the oral part of the examination and then the flight portion and for most, it will take between three and five hours of oral questioning and then maybe two in the plane. I had eleven hours of orals. I felt like I was drowning the whole time. He saw two things in me. He saw that I was a little bit insecure about the whole idea; I didn't have a lot of confidence in myself. And I think that he saw that I was female and he wanted to make sure that this was really what I wanted to do. And I have a really bad habit of thinking that I've kind of fooled somebody in getting where I'm at, that I don't really deserve to be here. And when you're face to face with someone and they're asking questions, even if you know the answer, it's pretty easy to get knocked out.

There's a lot of things that you do when you're training that are pretty scary. When I first started, I thought brave people just weren't afraid and I don't think that's the case now. I think brave people are just able to keep performing even though they are afraid. I think there's a lot of frightened people out there that just get through life somehow. Any physical skill, you can always keep improving. But the first couple of months that I instructed, I was thinking "My God, what am I doing here? I can barely handle this plane myself and I'm teaching somebody how to do it. Now I think that I'm a pretty good instructor because I have a lot of empathy. I don't know if it's being female but it's definitely being me, that I can bring a lot of patience to this job that a lot of other people don't have. 'Cause I like doing it.

A lot of people just instruct to build hours and ultimately, that's what I'm doing too, 'cause I want to work for an airline or something where I can make a little bit more money. I really don't make very much money. Last year, I made $12,000. Eventually I could be making a lot of money but I think that's really a lousy reason to do anything. I _can_ say that being really poor has made me more materialistic than I've ever been! I'd really like to be able to buy clothes but I wouldn't fly just because I made a lot of money.

There's a lot going on when you're flying. When you're flying in clouds that are very low and you're going to have to shoot an approach down the minimums and you're not sure if you can make it

into the airport on the first try, there's a lot to think about. You have
to have runway visibility of 200 feet and you have to have a half mile
overall visibility. They have radio navigation to help get you down to
that point. When you break out of the clouds at 200 feet above the
ground, and you're going slow at 100 or 150 knots, you have about 20
seconds to really get yourself oriented and get yourself locked on the
approach. You've got to get it down on the ground and slow and it's
got to be smooth and comfortable for Mr. CEO in the back. There's
a lot of teamwork and a lot of interaction.

I flew through a thunderstorm once and I thought that we were
going to...it was pretty scary. I wasn't an instructor yet. I was with an
instructor and we were flying at night and doing some training in the
clouds and all of a sudden it was pretty turbulent. It was raining really
hard and difficult to control the plane and there was lightning all over
the place. You just slow the plane down so that if you end up upside
down, it's not going to stress the plane. There's not really much you
can do. Thunderstorms are incredibly forceful.

I'll say things to my mother and I think they're pretty day-to-day
stuff and she gets all upset. I mean I've had engine failures and it just
doesn't bother me anymore. It's not that it's a daily occurrence, but it
has happened where I've had engine problems and that's what you
train for. I had one on takeoff and I was watching for other traffic
and the student had his hand on the throttle and it felt like he just
pulled it all the way back. And I turned to him and said, "Full
throttle!?" Like what are you doing? Twenty feet off the ground,
pulling the power back. So we just went straight ahead and landed. I
haven't had one at altitude.

Once I had a pretty bad cold and I couldn't breathe very well or
smell, and we were flying along and the low voltage light came on
which was telling me that we might have a problem with the
alternator, which isn't a big deal 'cause it's just for the radio and the
flaps. The engine ignition isn't dependent on the battery. We
recycled it and went through the check list again and it came on again
and I said obviously we have a problem with our alternator so we'll
just head back in, 'cause you don't want to lose your radio if you can
help it, especially around here 'cause it's busy. So about ten minutes
later we're almost into the airport and I start sniffing and say, do you
smell something? I was just so congested, I couldn't smell anything.
The reason that we were getting this low voltage light is that two
wires had shorted out and it spiked the alternator and kicked it off

line and kicked the whole electrical system off line. These two wires were smoldering in the engine compartment and I didn't smell it but obviously my student, who was white as a ghost, had been smelling it for the last ten minutes!

I think that in life there are different challenges, lessons that you have to learn because it always seems that in my life, I make the same mistakes a lot. I've gotten myself in the same kind of situations again and again and I just wonder if there's not recurrent themes. I like to think that there's something more and you don't just rot in the ground after you die. That scares me, if that's the end and that's it. Sometimes I feel like a little kid when there's company over and they don't want to sleep 'cause they don't want to miss anything. If there is an end, then I don't want to miss anything.

I think I was a pretty frightened kid. I was afraid of going into the deep end of the pool. I think flying and my training has really helped me a lot with that. Teaching helps because when the engine failed on takeoff, my student just kind of looked at me and I just realized that he wasn't going to do anything, that it was up to me to do something. He was looking at me as some kind of...instructor! That's when it really hit me what I was doing. It's kind of like being a life guard; it's all fun until you have to put your skills to the test.

We just keep training for emergencies, and train and train until hopefully it's automatic 'cause you don't want to have to think. I try to tell my students not to think, to think as little as possible in the plane. You want everything to be memorized and to have all kinds of aids available to help you. That's why we use check lists so we don't have to think, what do I have to do next? So hopefully, in an emergency, you've done it so many times that you do right again. That's like when I had that engine fire, and I got down on the ground and it was like a training exercise. When you got all done, it was just like every other emergency practice that we had ever done.

I've seen Top Gun a lot. I've seen it many times and it's a really terrible movie. It's really one of those stupid movies but you have to see it. You don't have a choice when you're a pilot, you have to know the lines from Top Gun! It's a macho field and an ego boosting kind of field. The people who are really unhappy are those who end up as flight instructors because it's the only way to build up your hours and they don't like people and interacting. I happen to really like teaching; not to say that I'm going to do it forever, but I really like it. I'm getting better about it but I know that I get more worried about someone being late. I don't know if the guys are just better at hiding it and they don't express it but if I had a student that was supposed to be back at 2--2:30 I start getting antsy and wonder where they are. I can see that nurturing thing because I have had a little hard time letting go of students. When they're ready to go, I sign them off but it's hard for me. I feel like I'm sending a kid off to college.

When I first started flying, I took the attitude that it doesn't matter if you're male or female but there are little things that I bring because I'm female and there's certain things that a male brings. I used to try really hard to be one of the guys, but it made no difference and now I am not sorry but I realize that I'm not one of the guys. Like when they sit around and burp, do dumb kinds of guy things, and it's not that funny and they're laughing. And now I get really excited about wearing girl clothes, like "Oh, I get to dress up!"

As a pilot, you're really dependent on your body. There's certain things that can go wrong with your body and if they do, then that's it. Like diabetes, that would be it, or serious heart trouble, low blood pressure. It would be difficult if I found out I had something like this, because I've put a lot of work, sweat and tears and my life into this. I know of a guy who got into a car accident; a drunk hit him and he lost an eye and that was it for him. I've spent a lot of money in training at this point, about $30,000 to get to be an instructor. In the back of your mind, you wonder what you would do. If you told me I could never fly a plane again, I'd have a hard time with that. If I wasn't doing this, I'd probably do something related to animals. I'd probably go back and either be a vet tech or something with animal activism. I try not to regret things that I have done. I'd rather regret something I did than something that I didn't do.

I go to a lot of high schools and talk to the kids about careers in aviation. I think it's important to encourage kids to pursue something and get them excited about doing something--anything. To realize that you shouldn't go through life on autopilot and go to a business school just because you're going to get a job and make x amount of money and that's the end of it. I mean, you're spending five days a week doing something that you're not thrilled about, so that you can have fun for two days of the week? That doesn't make sense. So you should be doing something that excites you. I definitely tell them to have outs; get a college degree, do <u>something</u>. I like to think that people aren't sheep. Hopefully we haven't gotten to the point where we're so stuck on immediate gratification. I didn't think that I'd be living in a roommate situation because I can't afford to live by myself, but that's the way it is and sometimes things turn out different.

Instructing is not really a career. Really, being an instructor is a stepping stone to something else. Unless I come back to it, nobody does this all their life. You can't, financially, and because it's somewhat stressful. I mean, I hope not, but eventually you're going to have a student who does something really stupid. It's funny, on any given day I'd probably say don't take up this career, don't do it! And another time, I'd say, oh it's great! Sometimes it gets frustrating when you see all these airlines going out of business, thinking, God, I may be working weekends for the rest of my life! But I like to think if someone is starting now, that hopefully the situation will be different in five years.

You certainly can't prepare your student for every situation that they're going to come up with. It is like being a parent. You give them the fundamentals and you give them an understanding of what's going on and why so that they can handle whatever comes up. And hopefully they have good enough judgment to make good decisions when things happen. A lot of it depends on somebody's judgment. I've had a couple of sixteen year old students and they pick up on the skill part of it really quickly but they have absolutely no fear, they have no concept that if they do something stupid, that might be the last stupid thing they do. They have no idea of their mortality. You have to be sixteen to solo and seventeen to get your license. I do think that's a real positive thing. I wish you could solo a little bit earlier and still not get licensed until you're seventeen.

I think it's hard to get a lot of kids to read. They're getting a lot of different subjects thrown at them that they might not otherwise be interested in. Here they are reading about physics and they don't even know it! That's why I'm so interested in talking to kids because I think that a lot of the problem with not knowing what you want to do and learn, and having no goals is that they don't know why they are in school. "Why am I learning this stuff, 'cause I don't even know what I want." But if you can give somebody something that's interesting, if I say you have to learn about aerodynamics or I'm not going to solo you, you're going to learn about aerodynamics. It's the law of effect. If you see a reason to learn it, you learn it! If you can get some kids that have no desire to learn English, to read about the history of aviation and write a paper on it, then that's a little bit more interesting. You can trick them into thinking that it's important to get an education.

I tell them what it's like to fly or what you can do when you fly. Like I can go to Block Island for the day and come back and it's no big deal. I even talk about the military 'cause I think that's even a good option for a lot of people. I believe that if you learn different things or you have different experiences, that they'll all come together and serve a purpose at some point. I wanted to travel and do something exciting and work as a team, teaching. You do use everything that you learn at some point, some obscure thing that I've learned has come back to help me.

It's calculated risk taking. If you take the chance that all this might work out, then it can. At one point in my training, I failed a test and I was pretty bummed about it. And someone, actually an older women who flies, sat me down and said, "Lynn, you tried and yea, you fell a little bit short but you'll get back on your feet and you'll get it next time. You're so much better off than most people who don't even try." I think that's the whole key--trying. You can't be a failure if you try. It might take you a little bit longer but don't worry about what other people think.

I'd like to think there's some meaning to life, that you aren't just put here for 50 years and then you die and that's it. I'd like to think that there is some purpose or that someone would remember me, that I did something--that I didn't waste it. What if there is judgment day and you get up there and you say well, I watched TV for 9000 hours of my life. There was nothing better, I was bored. You were bored? You couldn't think of anything to do? I can't imagine being bored. There's always something that I have to do yesterday.

Florinda
Human Rights Activist

I have friends who could plan their life! They're going to get married at a certain time or have this job, or work for this firm. I couldn't do that even if I wanted to, 'cause then I might as well be dead. You know exactly what you're going to do for the rest of your life. Maybe through my travels and meeting with different people, I saw that people can have very different lives. You have to be open to that because if you're not, it's always there but you don't see it.

Career professional human rights activist – interesting concept, working day after day, to help make human rights a reality. Not many people have the opportunity or the possibility of making this happen.

You have to be kind of open to the unknown. It's a little scary, 'cause you don't know what's there. If you look at your work as just a job, anybody can get a job doing something you get paid for. But can you do work that's satisfying, that you like, that's fulfilling? If your goal is monetary, that's fine too. You can identify a need, and you put in a certain amount of time. I always looked at time in terms of my work. This is my life, this is what I want to do.

I have always been interested in social justice issues or politics, and history and people and how they react to each other. I have a very strong background in science and math. That's my natural inclination, but I also have an interest in politics and history and as I was growing up, I examined the things that I was strongest in and also practical things. As I was getting older, I started thinking about what to do with history and politics. I was very interested in issues of Central America.

I wasn't going to be a politician. I didn't want to be a teacher, but I'm a practical person also. So, what am I going to do with this? I had a BS and I studied medical technology. I didn't want to be a doctor or a nurse. I decided I would go into medical research. I always had a strong sense of what I thought was politically correct and I was active as a volunteer.

When I was in college, the theory of science was really interesting to me, but then I started thinking, "What are you going to spend your life doing?" I'm a people person and I was thinking that I don't want to spend my days in a lab. The things that I do on a volunteer basis are things I'm really interested in. I'm tired at 6 or 7 o'clock when I go home and I don't want to go to a volunteer group meeting to do my politics. Wouldn't it be great to do what I'm really interested in as part of my work? And just the atmosphere in hospitals, in labs, in science, really lost its appeal to me.

I went to college right after high school, but I was always volunteering. During the summers as a teenager, I was a volunteer at the Museum of Science and on Sundays, I went to this elderly nursing home and wheeled patients to church. I went to visit them. When I was a little older, I belonged to a women's health collective and we did counseling. In undergraduate school, I did the big sister kind of thing, community development projects and working with kids, all as a volunteer.

At the end of my junior year, I studied sciences and philosophy. I went to a very small Catholic women's college in Vermont. That was in the middle seventies and it was really great, because it had a very small community of students and we talked about philosophy. Philosophy was a big core of the school. We wore hiking boots and we talked about philosophy. I like that environment, but then you start thinking about graduating, and "What am I practically going to do?".

I look at five to ten year slots. As a technologist, the money's really good, and you could always get a job somewhere else. What are you going to do with biology? What are you going to do with politics? This is practical. So I listened to my advisors. I would graduate, finish my degree and then do whatever I wanted to.

Medical technologists have to take a certification to belong to the professional society. I decided at that point, that I was not going to take it. I knew that if I continued along that path, it wouldn't propel me to really look into the things that I really wanted to do. It would have been very easy just to take the test and be certified. I didn't want to do that, so I decided not to but that meant that if what I wanted to do didn't work out, I would have missed an opportunity which translates into more money or a better position.

The first year I went home, I thought I wanted to do Public Policy or Law. Maybe I'd want to be a lawyer dealing with public policy. That would be the practical application of my interest. I didn't want to teach history; I didn't want a Ph.D.; I didn't want school anymore. I'd be a lawyer. So I was very fortunate; I got an internship in Boston at the Attorney General's Office, Consumer Complaints. Basically, I did Dispute Resolution and I learned a lot. I was there for about a year. It was a paid internship and that was the year that I was living at home, so I could afford to do that. With my background, I couldn't find anything paying a real salary.

That was a very good way to get experience and I felt that it's very important to do when you're young. It was very interesting for me. I handled individual consumer complaints and I dealt with people and lawyers in situations of resolving disputes so it can be a little touchy, but I'm very good at dealing with people. I'm the middle child, so I'm used to settling disputes.

Ultimately, I decided that I really didn't like working with lawyers and I didn't want to be a lawyer. The tasks are almost mechanical, like a lab. In theory, science is really interesting, but when you work in a laboratory, the practice of it is different.

I found I was really good at the scientific process, knowing how you look at things, how you dissect things, how you try to work things out. It's really useful in dealing with people and problems. So that's what I figured out many years later; I have a way of saying "Why is it this way?"

I got a job as a coordinator working in an elderly nutrition project and our job was to work in the community which started meal sites for low-income elderly people. It was an unpaid job but I worked for a year, got great recommendations and I showed them that I could work with people on a one-to-one basis in a social service setting. You're dealing with resolving disputes and finding solutions to people's problems. At that time also, an undergraduate degree was probably worth something. I think you needed that, but also my volunteer experiences throughout my high school years helped.

I moved here from Italy when I was about five years old. I grew up in a suburb where there weren't too many different kinds of people and the pressure was to really assimilate but being very young and having that very strong Italian connection, I had a different perspective. A lot of European societies were not individualistic societies. They're basically very practical. People were more together with the family. I had a conflict growing up in the US. thirty years ago. The mentality in the US was the big goal of getting your own apartment, be independent, have your own career, and leave your family. And a lot of people were doing that. A lot of women that I knew were thinking that way. You could be a doctor, a lawyer, or something else very high-powered. I feel those were the choices that we had. I mean, we thought we could do everything.

I decided at that time, that I really wanted to work on bigger issues. I wanted to work on public policy. I thought it was very important to work one-to-one, a personal level. It was very draining however, because when you are dealing with people in an immediate crisis and it's five or six o'clock, you don't necessarily go home. You have to deal with the crisis until it's over. It's very draining, but it's very rewarding in a lot of ways. And also as I looked at the issue, I was really interested in the macro picture. I was interested in poverty and public policy and social justice, why things happen to people. I was thinking of going back to get a Master's Degree and what I would be pursuing.

There were a number of programs in Public Policy, Public Administration and Community Development so I decided I would pursue a degree in Planning. I narrowed them down to a program that at that time was called Public Administration. I wanted to check out the Syracuse program because the Maxwell School of Public Administration was at Syracuse and I wanted to do an interdisciplinary.

I had an interview with the head of the department. I convinced him to give me the interview. What people see in black and white on paper is how they evaluate you for school or for jobs, and you have to be very articulate about what you can do and what you have done. But also, it was very important for me not to let other people classify me, and say, "Oh, you have this background, you can't do this." I went to other interviews in different universities and they were less open to my experience, or at least to giving me a chance. Basically, I was saying to them, "Listen, give me a chance. I'm paying for this. If I flunk, if I don't do well, it won't work out." I refused to take no for an answer. This particular guy was one of the heads of the department, and I convinced him to give me a chance. He liked what I had to say. He liked the fact that I was saying, "Give me a chance, I want to try" and I think he thought that I would make an industrious student and that I had the desire.

People who want a career in human rights always ask, "What should I study? What should I do?" In this kind of work, there are people from different backgrounds so it's very important to know what you want. It's also very important if you don't really know what you want, to know what you don't want and the more experience and exposure you have, you start finding out what's out there. For me, it was always, "I know I don't want to do this, but what's out there?" It's especially true when the job you want is nontraditional: human rights and development.

In graduate school, they have a lot of criteria. They want your money to an extent and they want you to finish X number of courses there. I also wanted to leave Syracuse for a while 'cause when you're in academics you have a weak perspective on the world. I could spend my life in academia, reading and meeting a lot of people. It's a very interesting program and I met a lot of people. It was also very conservative.

So everyone said, "You can't do that. You have to be accepted into a Harvard <u>program</u>." They didn't understand what I was trying to do. They said, "We've never done that." So I just kept going to different people and again, not taking "no" for answers, I said "This is what I want to do." It was sort of an untraditional approach to education. I was trying to get some practical experience and they didn't see where I could fit in.

So I was at some office in Harvard looking for a catalog of all the courses that they were offering the next semester, and I happened to overhear a person there talking to someone behind the desk about the program that she was in, and she said "No, I'm not matriculated at Harvard, but I'm taking courses," which was exactly what I wanted to do. I started talking to her and I said, "Who are you and what's this program?" She said her husband was in graduate school there and she wanted to take courses, but she wanted credit and there was a place in Harvard where you could apply to a particular school to get real credit. You could take the courses in matriculated programs. It's a big school and people did not know that. It was just a fluke. So that semester I went to Harvard and I worked it out with Syracuse that I would take this program and it would apply to my degree.

I wanted to go to Boston, because there was an organization there called Oxfam America. It's a development organization that I thought if I did development, that it was the type of development that I wanted to do. I always think of what I want to do and then try to find out where I can do it. I don't think in terms of a degree or in terms of a career. It's really the physical work; what will I be happy doing? Why do I want to do something I really hate? I'll find something out there. It's not that idealistic.

I think that you have to be true to yourself in what you want to do. Life isn't too short. You have to be practical, but you have to take risks. The hardest part for me was that I had a sense of what I wanted to do, but I could not articulate it because it didn't exist. And sometimes when it doesn't exist, you look like the outsider because you do know what you want but you haven't invented it yet. It's like, well who do you want to work for? Well, I don't know, who is out there? What are my choices? There might be something I never thought of.

Also at that time, I did a lot of traveling. I traveled through Europe a lot. I was interested in different people and cultures and travel and that exposes you to what's out there. Also, since I wasn't born in this country, I knew there was something beyond here. Discovery--what is out there. This is what I want to do and maybe I can make a living out of it. When you're younger, you have those options. You can make a list, but it's hard because you have family saying, "When are you going to get a real job?" or "What are you doing?"

It's easy to look retrospectively to see what you did and see how it fits into your life. But not so you can make the right choices, because sometimes there's a shorter distance between A and B, a straight line, but that's not how you really get there. There are also a lot of factors like why you want to live in a certain city and what your skills are. My life was not that methodical.

I started volunteering at Oxfam while I was taking the course in Harvard and working part-time as a Lab Technologist. That went on for a semester and then I went back to Syracuse and they told me I needed to take one more course. It was a stipulation. You had to finish your course work at Syracuse. In the meantime, I had decided that I wanted to do International Development work because of my experience with Oxfam and work overseas. I wanted to get some additional experience. I started thinking, "How am I going to get international experience?" And one thing that popped up was the Peace Corps.

I applied to the Peace Corps and in the meantime, I had to go back to Syracuse to take my course and I kept my job in Boston. It's a "catch twenty-two" with development. You have a Master's, that's fine. Do you have practical experience? Have you ever lived in another country? I had the theory, but now I needed the practical experience. My job was very good at the hospital, and I wanted to keep it because I was going to graduate and it was summer and I wasn't going to hear from the Peace Corps until September so I didn't want to give up this part-time job. At that time, it was really cheap to commute from Syracuse to Boston, so I commuted. I lived in Syracuse and to keep my part-time job, I only had to work every other weekend. I was making enough money just to pay for the transportation, 'cause the purpose of keeping that job through the summer was to give me an option. They allowed me to do that because I asked them. If you don't ask, you will never know.

I got into the Peace Corps and went to Senegal. I was assigned to do Community Health work. Although I had some qualms about the Peace Corps, it was a very positive experience and I met some very interesting local people. I learned a lot about development because in Senegal, everybody was there, the Russians, the Italians, the French, doing development. So I got a real sense of what development on a non-grassroots and a grass roots level was like.

When I left the Peace Corps, I went back home. I needed time to adjust and because I had volunteered in Oxfam, I knew about the organization and I had liked it and there was a position open on a project called the Fast For World Harvest. It was sort of an entry level position. My qualifications were kind of beyond that, but I wanted to take it also because for people who work on the nonprofit level, it's very competitive so you have to be willing to take any kind of job. You have to take your opportunities as they come.

Through my work with OXFAM, I realized that my interest in development is not in the field, not overseas work. It's really working in this country doing Public Policy, doing advocacy. I was there for 4 1/2 years. I started working with the person who is the Public Policy person, doing education and policy. Development is a very interesting thing, but personally I changed in what I wanted to do.

The people that you work with overseas on human rights issues are the same people that development agencies work with, that is, people who are organizing for basic human needs. I happened to be working on hunger related issues, but it's very interconnected. I didn't know that at the time, but the public policy and advocacy work that we did was basically human rights. You can't divorce fulfilling basic human needs from hunger or shelter. You can't take people out of the context of the world they're living in, and what's happening to them as citizens of their country.

Say we're working on a project in a certain country and we're funding the local women's cooperative and it sounds very ideal. Well, in some countries that's a very political thing to do and those people, just for organizing and coming together to try to change their lot, put themselves in danger by their own governments.

Some people in the third world developing countries live under very repressive situations. You think, "Why didn't this project work? We gave you the money. All you had to do is get together and build the well. What's the problem?" The problem is that just coming together to do that in this particular country where all these political situations are coming together, can be perceived as radical or they're related to someone else who has been arrested. It's very connected. That's why some aid programs don't work. That's what keeps people poor--politics. People aren't poor because they're stupid. They don't have access to resources sometimes, because there are obstacles that are put there to keep them that way. So you see it because you're dealing with individual lives and they're affected by everything. Their country and their lives are affected by everything around them. It is a small world in a sense and there is an interconnectedness in terms of politics and human rights.

On a personal level, I wanted a change. I wanted more responsibility. A position came up in Amnesty International and I thought it sounded a lot closer to what I was really interested in. This is the job I have now, which is Deputy Regional Director and I don't see this as the end of my career either. It was interesting when I worked at Oxfam. That was the kind of work where I felt it's not just a job. I liked going into work everyday. I liked what I was doing. It really reflected my politics and who I was, particularly in development and you can't find a lot of those jobs.

Amnesty International is a worldwide organization that is nonpartisan and supported only by its members. It works for basic human rights for all people plus an end to torture and executions.

I thought that if I ever got a job like that, I could stay there for years and years. It meets all your needs, but you change and your needs change. For me, I needed more challenges because I don't see my work as a job. It might manifest itself in another way, another organization. I don't always know what I want, because I don't know what the other opportunities are and I could have another forty or fifty years of work left in me. I think I'm going to go through many different transitions along the way.

I'm in charge of membership development services in the Northeast. It's a volunteer organization and we have members all over the country and all over the world. The members who belong to Amnesty are the activists, they do the work, they make Amnesty happen. We're always looking for people who are interested in human rights and we help them learn what the various mechanisms are about and provide the activists with resources that they need to do their work. There are some basic responsibilities in terms of what's needed for the membership with training and starting new local groups or speaking publicly and networking in the community. I'm both, an activist and doing my job.

It's hard when people say, "What's your job? What's your position?" I guess my profession is now an activist. I happen to work for Amnesty International. To me, it's not so much a question of loving what I want to do, but to do advocacy work or political activism or social justice work. I could spend 24 hours a day doing that. The more of me that I'm working with and knowing about, the more effective I am because I become more knowledgeable and the more people who talk to me and the more experience I have, the more effective I am towards my goal which is social justice. I'm also fortunate that I like my job.

Amnesty has a responsibility to people who give money to make sure that we do the work that we're supposed to be doing. It's not because we're a bunch of "do gooders," we <u>care</u> about human rights in the world. We're a multi-million dollar a year organization that people put their trust in and they expect that their money will be spent correctly, to do the work effectively. So on a professional level, that's also very important. Personally, it's also very rewarding, because I'm able to spend time doing what I think is important in the world and that gives me personal satisfaction.

When I worked in a lab, it was easy to distinguish when I was taking work home with me. When you're dealing with people and you're an advocate for something, you don't stop at a certain time, so sometimes it blends and sometimes it doesn't. It's not just that I have an interest in Amnesty or human rights; I'm not only representing an organization that I believe in, but it's a part of myself too. So people also make that personal connection. People can know that torture is bad, but why they should work with your issue is also a personal connection. They like how Amnesty operates; they like what you do. They also like you. You put yourself on the line. If I'm unethical, that's a reflection of the organization, particularly if I'm representing what a lot of people consider such a moral thing, like human rights. It's hard to separate yourself and do something totally out of character or be unethical.

It's not a nine to five job. You're working with volunteers, and people meet after they work. Their job is sometimes after work or on the weekends, or there is a crisis and they're in a position of dealing with the Haitian issue, or whatever, or you're doing a Regional Conference or training. You might be very intense at one time and then you have a lull. So it might be nine to nine for a couple of weeks. The organization recognizes that you're a human being and as an activist, people don't watch the clock to see when you are five minutes late. In other organizations, you have to be in at nine o'clock and you have to be out at a certain time. People recognize this, so the time is flexible. If I'm really tired staying up all night working for a meeting, I can come in late. We also get 3 or 4 weeks vacation; we're pretty well compensated. If I work on the weekend, I get comp. time. When you take it is a different matter but I personally feel it's important to take a chunk of time off. If I need to take a day off, I take a day off because it can get really crazy.

Nonprofits vary and one of the biggest things is getting the resources to do what you want to do and also to have a life. We don't have extravagant salaries, but Amnesty as an organization, realized that we have professional people and we have to compensate them with health insurance, etc.. We want people who are going to be with us for a long time, not just a couple of years. In a lot of organizations, if you're young you're willing to take less money if it's a good cause. You can't afford to do that in this society anymore, in this country. As an organization, both management and staff feel that's important. We can have a normal professional job and a life. On that level, it's a job.

I've been very fortunate; I've worked for every organization that I've wanted to, in both development and human rights that are very well respected in their fields. I'm very fortunate to have done that. It is possible to do, but part of it was luck, being at the right place at the right time. Also taking risks is important and there might be some things you have to put off to get experience, but you try it. If you really want to do something, you want to try it. It's very scary because you might fail, but that shouldn't stop you from going for something. You don't know if your art work or what you want to do is going to work out. It could be very easy. You could fall into a pattern where you get this degree and get this job and you get compensated.

You need to support yourself, feed yourself. That's very important, but you have to take risks and sometimes you fail. You can't be afraid of that, and you can't say no. You can't accept other people saying no for you.

When you're younger, you hear, "What do you want to be when you grow up?" Well, you don't know what you want to be, but you know what you want to be doing. You know what you like. You have to be really true to yourself and you have to be open to other avenues that you might not have ever thought of before. And when it comes to a job, it might be possible, might not. It looks like risk, but it's not. If you're doing something that you love or you take the chance, then you have a fifty-fifty chance of winning and losing. It's not really a risk. It's like the glass theory--is it half empty or half full? You can look at it as being half full.

Into It

Jim
Economist, Low Income Housing

I went through a period when I was much younger, which was very philosophical trying to figure out with pure logic and basic observation, what's worth doing. And you can't do it. With pure logic, you can't even figure out if you exist. And it wasn't an idle intellectual exercise; it was a very important basic search for who I was and what I was going to do

and I was, at times, very unhappy and desperate for the answer. And what I finally came to was, you can't figure it out but there are some things that when you do them, they're self-justified. I can't tell you why they feel worthwhile to do. I don't believe in God. I don't believe in an after life. I believe that when you die you're dead, that basically, you're meat and bones that somehow figured out how to think.

I don't have mythical or spiritual answers for what the purpose of life is, or why we should do certain things, or what makes something worthwhile or not. But I do have strong feelings and I learned that what I have to do, is not figure them out. I have to learn to listen to them and to observe myself. When I do this, I feel like what I'm doing is worthwhile and it gives me energy. When I do <u>that</u>, it feels like I'm wasting my time. It makes me worry about how long I'm going to live when I do that. So I'm not going to do that anymore. I'm going to do this other thing where the question of "is this worthwhile?" doesn't occur to me very often. It <u>feels</u> worthwhile. The answer is--what's worth doing is something that comes out of your gut that you are somehow born with or got inbred early. You've got to find that thing. You can't figure it out.

When I began working out of my home, it wasn't a deliberate long term calculated plan. I think if you had asked me at any point before I did it, I would have said that it would be wonderful and it was maybe a dream, but I didn't think it would work. The way it happened was I had just reached the end of my tolerance in my job and I had to leave it for my own sanity. I looked around at what other possibilities there might be and just decided that I would try, figuratively, hanging up my shingle and say "Hey, I'm a consultant in this business for hire" and set an hourly rate and see if I got any business. And so, it happened. That was a very short time span, going from not believing it was practical to trying it and liking it.

I call myself a development consultant. My clients are nonprofit organizations and sometimes government entities concerned with affordable housing development and community development in low-income neighborhoods. The biggest part of my work is helping nonprofit organizations to develop specific projects where we acquire a group of land parcels and put together the funding to build new housing or will acquire deteriorated existing buildings and put together the financing to rehabilitate them. It involves many different aspects like the actual real estate mechanics of acquisition and the financing mechanics of structuring loans, grants and equity investments. It also involves planning for the long-term management of the projects, things like how the residents will be selected. It turns out to be a very controversial and complicated matter just to select who the families will be who get to live in the housing that we develop.

A lot of these things involve a high degree of technical skills. Some of them involve a lot of institutional knowledge about programs and much of it involves communication skills, persuasive skills and negotiator skills. It's just a lot of being able to go back and forth between different organizations, funding sources, land owners, regulators and try to work out solutions to a million different problems and specialized circumstances that pertain to a particular project. The problem is that it's fundamentally a public piece of business. It's fundamentally government and the government has withdrawn from it.

The government subsidizes middle-class and rich people's housing to the tune of billions of dollars a year, but the idea that we would spend anything like that for poor people's housing is anathema and we don't do it. People are allowed to deduct interest on mortgages of up to a million dollars on two houses and think it's their birthright. You can't deduct any other consumption expenditure, how come we get to deduct interest on our mortgages?

I was Executive Director of an organization called The Boston Housing Partnership. It's a nonprofit organization serving the whole city of Boston. Nonprofit just means that whatever surplus the business might generate is recycled into additional charitable purposes, rather than going into somebody's pocket as profit. In nonprofit, you certainly have paid employees and you can certainly make money on real estate deals. You can charge fees for your services, but you don't have stockholders who receive dividends.

This organization was started in the early eighties when the federal government, under Reagan, really cut back on money for affordable low-income housing. The idea was to bring together on one board of directors, all of the top decision makers who have to agree to make something big happen for the troubled neighborhoods. So, we had the presidential chairmen of the biggest banks in town and some of the smaller ones and we had the heads of all the city departments who deal with housing and then we had the representatives of a good sampling of neighborhood based nonprofit organizations. We also had a sprinkling of respected "do gooder" types in academics. We put together large scale programs. We'd do five hundred housing units like this, do a thousand housing units like that and smaller nonprofit organizations would apply to the program to take over the units. For the ones that were selected, we would put together the financing and for the financing sources, we would reduce the perceived risk because we were there, overseeing and backing up these organizations.

It's not my element really, and it is full of conflict. There's millions of dollars involved sometimes and that can make people into real monsters at times. It's like street fighting, only with a tie on. I did that for five years; it was a good step but in the winter of '91, I kind of hit the wall. I said, "Hey, I just can't keep doing that, so it's time for somebody else. I've had enough." I had brought one very large, multi-year program that involved a huge fight with the Federal Government (HUD), to a successful conclusion and the next program was pretty well launched so in a sense, it was a logical time.

I came to Boston to teach economics. I was a brand new Ph.D., had a job at Brandeis and had never been to Boston in my life. I landed here and started looking around for a house to rent. There weren't many houses to rent, so I bought a house in Dorchester which was an economically depressed, integrated neighborhood where you could, at that time, buy a beautiful big old Victorian house for $30,000 or less. And the way I like to live is to put together a communal household of between five and eight people, so I needed a big house. I had done that before and I like it to be in a neighborhood where people of different races can be comfortable.

I started looking for ways to get involved, because the neighborhood really appealed to me and yet I could see it had terrible problems. There were a lot of boarded up houses, a lot of businesses going out of business, a lot of trash-strewn vacant lots, a lot of houses burning every night, cars burning, that kind of thing. So I had the dream of "Hey, we get together with neighbors and we do something about this!"

As it turned out, some other people had just started an organization called Dorchester Bay Economic Development which was to be a nonprofit real estate development organization to get ownership of abandoned houses and fix them up, sell them at affordable prices and try to do things in the retail district to bring better stores into the shopping district, spruce the place up generally. And there was also a neighborhood association which had no staff and very little budget, totally made up of volunteers. They had started it just a few months before I moved to the neighborhood and I started going to their meetings. Then I was elected by my local neighborhood association to represent them on the board. At that time, we had one staff person.

Our projects would consist of one house at a time, and we'd talk about that one house all night. My involvement started as a volunteer serving on the Board of Directors, first as a member and then as Director. The Director is an unpaid, elected position, a community resident who volunteers to give some time to oversee the organization and guide its major policy decisions, give it legitimacy and see that it really serves the interests of the neighborhood.

During one of the first meetings I went to, the local Kreskie 5 & 10, one of the major buildings in the shopping district had just shut down. It wasn't a big shopping district in the neighborhood, but there was this big building and a year before, the only supermarket in the neighborhood had gone out of business. The idea was to buy the Kreskie building and see if we could get a food store to open up in it.

So people had gone to the city and gotten a hundred thousand dollar grant and had gotten Kreskie to agree to sell the building for a hundred thousand dollars. At this meeting, the Executive Director, the only paid staff reported to the board that when she went to the closing with Kreskie to take title to the building and the papers were signed and the representative of Kreskie was reaching across the table to hand her the keys to the building, the local Ward Boss, the political appointee of the Mayor who was also sitting at the table, grabbed the keys saying "I'll take those. We really control this deal" and he walked out of the room. And so, there we were. The Ward Boss had essentially said that he was going to make a mockery out of this organization, and we were just going to be a shell. He would pick who would come in to operate it and what would happen. We all sat there and heard this report from our Executive Director. I raised my hand and said, "I move we call a locksmith and change the locks." The Executive Director said, "Oh no, we can't do that. We've got to play ball with them." I said, "No. Bullshit" and the board agreed and that's what we did.

We changed the locks and we faced this guy down. He was just a bully. There's a sequel to that story. The heating system went in building next to it and was abandoned by its owner. It was a four story building with a drugstore on the ground floor. The city took it for nonpayment of taxes and put out a request for proposals. They would have developers write proposals to the city for how they would redevelop this building and what businesses they would put in it.

This character shows up in the neighborhood driving a black Lincoln, wearing blue jeans and a black turtle neck and gold chains saying that he's going to put a Steak House on the roof and all these fancy businesses in this building. It just stunk to me--obviously a fraud. We just wanted the drug store company that operated on the ground floor to get the building because it was a nice, down-to-earth, legitimate business serving neighborhood needs. This same Ward Boss was trying to manipulate the process in favor of this guy. There was a public meeting and I can't even remember all the names he called me at that meeting.

One day I come down to breakfast and opened my Boston Globe and there's the Ward Boss being hauled away in handcuffs. It turns out that this guy in the black turtle neck got himself wired for sound by the FBI and got the Ward Boss on tape demanding a kickback for fixing the deal for him. The guy had actually wanted to develop the building. This was an assumed name that the FBI had given him in the Witness Protection Program, because he had done something else in Arizona and now he tries to come in and set himself up as a developer in Boston. And the first thing you know, a

Ward Boss is trying to put the squeeze on him and he goes back to the FBI and does it all again.

The Boston Housing Partnership had just been formed and announced this incredible program where they were going to give us money to go out and buy all the worst buildings in our neighborhood. It would even give us money ahead of being accepted into the program, so that we would have staff money to put our proposal together. Also included in the money for the proposal was earnest money, to tie up buildings. So when we would put up a proposal, we would have already used their money to pay our staff to put the proposal together and used their money to get building owners of slum property to sign Purchase of Sale Agreements. Then, if we put together a good proposal, the Boston Housing Partnership would provide the financing to actually do the rehab. It was an amazing, incredible thing 'cause up to then, we had gotten nothing but trouble from downtown and the occasional crumb. Suddenly this new organization is announced and we thought it was great and so I went on staff to put together our proposal.

I was really taking a pay cut and taking a job with much longer hours. I put that project together and saw it through. When that project was in construction and mostly built, the Executive Director of Boston Housing Partnership came to me and said, "I'll be sixty-five years old pretty soon; I'm looking for someone who's going to do this next. How'd you like to be that person?" I said, "You got to be kidding." But he wasn't. I did not at all think of myself as the next Executive Director of The Boston Housing Partnership. I wasn't even Executive Director of Dorchester Bay. I was a Project Manager and I'd been in Boston all of five years at that point, and still thought of myself as learning the ropes. But he and others saw something in me that led them to think I could do that.

I desired to do that and in some ways, it was a mistake. In some ways it wasn't. I absolutely loved working for Dorchester Bay. The office was a two block walk from my house. It was a job where, although I worked incredibly hard, I didn't feel like I was at work. I felt like I was living. It was just a part of my life. Someone was paying me to do what I wanted to do passionately.

I love to fix things and I love to build things and I long for community and here I was fixing and building for a community that I cared a lot about and that I lived in. So that meant a tremendous amount to me and it uses all my skills. I have good math skills; I have good communication skills, I have building skills and I like dealing with people of different cultures. It brought all that together in one job.

All this housing that I had just developed was rental housing and the history of low-income housing is that it gets developed and then it fails. The maintenance isn't kept up and you get bad tenants in there and you get drug problems and I didn't want to see that happen. I could see that however dedicated Dorchester Bay might be, we were going to need a backstop. This Boston Housing Partnership was going to be as important to the survival of the project I had just developed and the other nine projects like it across the city, as the actual neighborhood organizations that developed them.

So I saw it as a really important mission and I did have that dream of being the leader of an organization, so I took the job at Boston Housing Partnership and I never enjoyed it. I always felt that it was important work, that I was doing good stuff, but it has an office downtown and you have to have a lot of interaction with people in the...I don't know what the right word is, but it's that other culture where people think it's just normal to work in tall buildings and wear suits. I can't totally explain it, but I just have a real allergy to that. I kept thinking I would get used to it and it would go away, but it just got worse.

As Executive Director, you're responsible for the complete day-to-day management of the organization and the hiring and supervision of the staff. You sign all the checks; you're responsible for moving all the programs along. Whenever staff underneath you gets stuck, you've got to intervene in some way to either coach them or step in. You've also got to manage the board, since the board members are all volunteers and it's not full-time for them, yet they set the policy for the organization. You've got to define the options; you've got to bring proposals to them. All the practical work of keeping all the various board committees going, including the monthly board meetings, is your responsibility.

And it's a lot of meetings. That was another thing that was a real shock. I found that in every job, there is something that you do a disproportionate amount of, that bends your personal life out of shape. If you're a postman and you walk a mail route, then you probably don't want to go for a walk at all when you get home. When I was a teacher, I went out of my way to make an atmosphere where people would feel comfortable asking questions and tried to be very good at answering them in a way that would be both informative and make you glad you asked. When I got home, I didn't want to be asked a question about anything from anyone. After a while with BHP, when the day was filled with meetings and I got home, I did not want to have a meeting about anything and that's really hard, because I live in a cooperative living situation and one of the very basic things about making those work is to get together regularly and maintain communication; talk about small problems before they get to be big problems. I had always been an advocate for that. Suddenly, I was a person who could hardly sit still for a house meeting, because I had been in meetings all day.

A major program that I had to deal with upon arriving at Boston Housing Partnership involved about a thousand apartments in about fifty apartment buildings. These were all buildings that were originally built as middle-class or even higher-class apartment houses around the turn of the century, but the neighborhoods had gone downhill.

In the seventies, right after the riots, the federal government was looking around for something it could do quickly and make some headlines, just the way they are now out of the LA riot, to show that they are doing something about urban problems. They found three white, for-profit developers and quickly put together this package of buildings and financed a kind of a slapdash, cosmetic rehab. They got their picture in the paper, made a lot of money for these developers and within a few years, the buildings were run-down and the developers were going on to other things.

The gas bills and the taxes were unpaid. The mortgages had been insured by the Federal Government and they were now foreclosing and because we had a "Free Market" Republican administration, their idea was that you foreclose, and then you sell the buildings to the highest bidder. Of course, that's the way the free market works. The Boston Housing Partnership organized a coalition of the Democratic political leaders, the Republican bank presidents, local business leaders and the neighborhood nonprofits like the one I came out of, to say to HUD, "No, you're not going to do this. We will take over as many of these buildings as we can as nonprofits and you're going to provide adequate subsidy to do the job right this time." The Federal Government's first response was, "Fine, we'll give you the buildings for a dollar." And we said, "No. You give us the buildings for a dollar <u>and</u> adequate subsidy continuing for at least the next fifteen years to run them properly."

They needed to be subsidized. Poor families can afford to pay one hundred or two hundred dollars a month. That doesn't even keep oil in the tank and janitors in the hall, much less pay a mortgage and we needed big mortgages to pay for all the repairs that these buildings needed. They needed everything from roofs to windows to boilers.

Subsidy is additional rent from the government needed to supplement what the tenant can afford to pay. We estimated that in order to do the job right and have the buildings serviced long term, it would cost close to nine hundred per month, per apartment. Even getting the buildings for free, because they needed about fifty thousand dollars an apartment in repairs plus the architects and engineers fees and the staff time involved and all the other, what are called "self costs," the amount comes to more like sixty or seventy thousand dollars per apartment. The mortgage payments on seventy thousand dollars were about five or six hundred dollars a month and then you needed another four hundred a month for utilities and janitors and ongoing maintenance. So the economics of rental housing are surprising to people and at least in Boston, nobody builds a new building to rent, certainly not to rent to poor people, but not even to rent to middle-class people. All rental housing is existing older buildings and they were built in another era.

All these projects where people from a church take a week off from their jobs and build a house for a poor family, it's a wonderful experience for them; it's wonderful for the family who gets the house, but this is a large-scale problem. It requires a large scale response and it's not just housing that's affected. Housing is where I happen to make my particular contribution, but what I'm really working on is the poverty problem and the urban problem. These are really dysfunctional neighborhoods. It's not just the housing that's broken down in these neighborhoods; it's the schools and the businesses and the economy and the delivery of basic city services.

So HUD screamed and fought and tried to portray us in every possible bad light and we kept at them. You write letters, you fly down to Washington and have these awful meetings with them. You fight battles in the newspapers where they say things and you say, "That's not quite the way it is." Once you get into the press, it's so out of control and reporters never understand and get it right, so it's a shot in the dark as to whether you're shooting yourself in the foot or the person you aimed the shot at.

The incredible strength of the Boston Housing Partnership was that we had rich republican bankers on our side, rich, well connected republican businessmen who could call people in the White House and say, "No, this is how it should be done in Boston." Somehow, they could keep their republican ideology but at the same time, be on the right side of this particular issue. As long as we didn't talk about bigger issues, we were allies. And maybe they were only doing it, because it buys them peace on the home front. All I can say is that they were good strong allies for this battle.

Ultimately, all those people that we were fighting at HUD were the same deal, just like the Ward Boss; one day you pick up the newspaper and they're all indicted. At the same time that they were telling us that the money we wanted was too much and all this should be turned over to the free market and all these programs that they were administering should be dismantled, they were cutting sweet deals with wealthy contributors to funnel subsidies to them on their projects, where they could make big profits. So we got those buildings and we got adequate funding. We got more money than anyone dreamed was possible in the 1980's to build low-income housing. It was a very tough battle.

Most people don't understand what an economics education is. They think of it as some branch of business. Economics is not business. It's very much an academic discipline like anthropology or physics, trying to discern basic laws about things and most of the time, it's very abstract. You're trying to boil down incredibly complicated human phenomena to a couple of lines on a graph and come out with generalizations that would be true in an amazingly large variety of circumstances. I think it has some real wisdom to impart, so I think I did learn a lot from the formal study in economics. I think also it has a lot to do with temperament, aptitude and basic skills.

I grew up in a household where there were very interesting dinner table conversations going back for as long as I can remember. A child was always welcome to participate at whatever level he could participate at and accorded respect by my parents and whatever guests we had, including my older siblings and whatever guests they had. I don't feel like I was talked down to, or that my opinions were not listened to, or made fun of. I think that happens a lot to kids.

People don't communicate the expectation that kids can participate in serious conversation when they're seven and so they don't. In my household, it was the reverse.

My father was a very knowledgeable and thoughtful man and so is my mother. He was a very interesting person to have a conversation with and a good listener and in fact, a man of few words. He had to feel that you really wanted him to say something for him to speak. He was quite happy not to say anything and I think probably, a lot of people have the experience of growing up having parents talking at them a lot and they shut them out. I didn't have that problem. My experience was always drawing him out, wanting to learn more from him.

In the seventh grade, I had a social studies teacher who taught about the great depression and that the New Deal and FDR were all a sham and a fake. I would come home and I'd ask my father about it and he would give me the other side of it, so I'd go back and argue with my teacher. That was a great way to begin to learn about macro-economics.

During my first job, I reached a point one day riding home on the commuter train where I said, "I've had enough. I'm going to go back to school and study something hard and really important and it's going to give me a whole new career." And what's that going to be? I remembered all those dinner table conversations about FDR and the great depression and it was then 1975, the Arabs had just cut off the flow of oil and inflation had just turned to 12 per cent. Economics seemed really important again so I thought, "It'll be economics." But I had my fill of math in high school. I didn't take a single math course in college and I only took two economics courses, so it was a bit of a stretch 'cause economics has become extremely mathematized. Everything is expressed in calculus and I hadn't had any.

When I got my next vacation I took two weeks off, sat in a chair and I had a couple of economics textbooks that a friend of mine gave me and I read them. I took the graduate record exam in economics and I scored in the 90th percentile, so I got into Cornell with a full tuition grant the first year and assistantships from then on. I did three years of course work instead of the usual 2 because when I arrived on campus, I had to sneak over to the undergraduate math department and take calculus 101. Then, I took a year off because I got this amazing job in Washington.

One day I saw something on a bulletin board about the president's Council Of Economic Advisors looking for people who had finished their course work for their Ph.D. to come to Washington and serve as staff for the council. I was 28 at the time and I applied. When I called them up, I said, "I'd like to come down and talk to you" and they said, "That's really not necessary; we don't do in-person interviews for these jobs. We just go by the written application and the recommendations." And I said, "I'd like to come down and talk to you; I'll do it at my expense." So they said, "O.K.." I think that probably made an impression.

I was Junior Staff Economist for Labor Market Policy. I worked one-on-one with the senior staff for labor and then sometimes with the three actual council members. I was working day and night and often writing memos to the members of the council and getting back comments from them and they were waiting for me to run stuff on the computer and come back and give them results; that was terrific. That was a complete breakdown of routine and all red tape, but as soon as things got a little bit slow, the routine would come to the foreground and then I just became totally allergic to it. I don't feel comfortable, I don't feel energized, I feel depleted at the end of the day. Life is kind of grey. Work is prison. Work is not living and so living is the weekend, vacations, sometimes it's evenings, but usually I'm depleted too much. Then I'm in that mode where work is work and it's not living and all pleasure has to be crammed in around the edges.

Satisfaction doesn't come out of necessarily achieving all the goals, because the goals are really huge when you think of them, like taking the poor inner-city neighborhoods and turning them into good places. Whatever successes you have in the process of working toward the goal is good, but the important thing is, it feels good to be working toward that goal. I've learned the earmarks of things that have that feeling, that create that feeling for me.

Things that pertain to building a community tend to be things that feel very worthwhile to me. In fact, a great range of things where I'm working as part of a team toward a shared goal feel worthwhile to me. One of the things that really turned me off about academics, that really shocked me once I got deeply into it, was that I assumed that most researchers, academic people, were primarily concerned with solving the great questions in their field, or advancing the state of knowledge in that field for its own sake. That's what gave them energy and that when you're an economist, you and the other economists felt like you were a team working toward producing greater clarity about economic principles in economic practice policies. It's not that way. Most academics are primarily concerned with the project of building their careers. And it's very distressing; it's intensely, personally, competitive in academics.

When you find the person who just loves to talk after hours about the subject and is delighted with a new perspective on something as much as if he thought of it, that's the rare individual. Most of them would rather talk about the latest paper, what that does for the person who wrote it in terms of a career move, rather than what that paper really means for the state of options in the field. That's the feeling that I got in academics and it drove me screaming from the field. But I find that in my present field, there are a lot of people I can work with who are motivated as I am with wanting to fix things and who want to try to make some really awful living conditions better. So that keeps me up, being part of a team where the team is goal oriented and the people are not terribly ego-driven.

Accept what your feeling tells you. If it tells you that working on cars is what gives you joy, then by God, work on cars. If it tells you that being a forest ranger is what would give you joy, even though you grew up in the city and you only saw a forest for the first time when you were ten years old in the Boy Scouts or something, be a forest ranger. That's the wisdom. Another thing more down-to-earth is to consider the nonprofit sector. I didn't until I was 25 years old and I was a pretty well informed person, but it didn't really penetrate that there was a nonprofit sector in this economy that has many good jobs in it.

Into It

Zyra
ESL Teacher

I have a lot of friends who are retired and they love it, and you know what they do? They have these two-for-one vouchers and they're always going to the theater. They take courses at schools which they only audit. I don't like to sit and be entertained. I like to play bridge, but I must be active. I like the movies, but I really have learned about myself and I probably have even more potential hidden somewhere that got stifled when I was young.

Zyra represents one of those combinations of compassion – learned through experience – and concern – expressed through a desire to help and to do something positive. And learning to combine these with a personal need to remain useful and vital.

I know that life is not forever. Death is very real to me. I lost a brother at the age of fifty-five and my parents died rather young. The next ten years of my life are vitally important because I'm getting older and yet I'm young enough and I still have my health. Who knows what will be in ten years? So I value "It's either now or never." That's why I want to retire. I'm not enjoying my job anymore and why should I spend my days doing that same thing? I want to enjoy it and get satisfaction, otherwise I'm not going to do it.

I never dreamt that I could really have as good a career as I have had. I made very good money. I'm going to take early retirement and I am really nervous about it. I've been thinking about it for a long time now. When I used to tell people that I think I'm going to do this English as a second language and that I think I'm going to take early retirement, I always said, "but look I don't know what I'm really going to do." I would always have to end it like that. I'm anxious, because money's been no problem for a long time and my income is going to be very different. But I went over my finances with a financial advisor and all that crap and I'm just going to do it. That's where I have the confidence based on past experience, that it's going to work out.

I went to college; I was a wonderful student. I was supposed to be. When I was a kindergarten teacher, my first job, I could not handle it emotionally. I graduated college; I wasn't even 19 years old, and I was a baby. I was used to being a good little girl. I come from what I consider an intelligent typical middle income family. I was the youngest and kind of protected and there I was out of college teaching kindergarten children and for the first time I had to be in front of this class. They were kindergarten kids and I could not handle it. I gave up and went to secretarial school and became a secretary. My first secretarial job was in 1951, and in 1958 I got a job with the Port Authority of New York as a secretary. I went to therapy which helped me a lot. I was going to this psychiatrist who said he thought this was the best secretarial job and a very wonderful job for me, because I needed a protected environment.

In 1959 my mother died and that really left me alone, because I was very dependent on her. I was 31 and I thought I was the kind of person who should have fallen apart and not be able to handle it, but within a year I managed and functioned very well and certainly was much more capable of taking care of myself than I realized.

I continued working at the Port Authority and I used to hear, particularly from these two women who sat near me, about how many more years they had to retire. I knew I hated it and when I thought, God, I have eighteen years until I retire, I knew I had to do something about it. The thought was making me very depressed. The average person of forty doesn't go from becoming a secretary to computer programmer.

One of the things I did was I went to NYU and took a battery of aptitude tests for two days. When you're out of school for a long time you lose your confidence; you don't know your ability. That was wonderful, because I got a good report on that. I was competing with young college graduates for this and I came out with a very high score which made me feel I still had a bit of a brain, even if I wasn't using it. Then I looked into what career was practical to go into and computer programming was a very open field then and they needed people.

Actually, they suggested that I be a pharmacist or a librarian at that point. I knew I was going there with the idea of becoming a programmer. That few days of testing gave me a renewed confidence which I sort of lost when I was a secretary. I was always apologetic about it, you know. I'm a secretary, but making everyone know I was a college graduate. I always had to throw that in. I knew it was an Achilles heel. I didn't feel proud of it.

The Port Authority had an educational refund program and at the time, you could become a programmer. You could become a trainee with just a college degree. I went and applied for this course, because I felt that if I were trying to get into a new field at that age, I had to have more than the minimum requirement especially if you're working with a handicap, and being forty was a little bit of a handicap. I went to NYU and they had a very interesting basic computer course that wasn't on a real computer. It was a make believe computer. The whole thing was verbal. We started out with twenty-five students, a lot of young people. By the end of the term, every time he introduced a new programming concept, we lost people. There were nine people left at the end of the term and I got an A in the course, so I thought I could do it. Then I went and took another course at NYU.

I applied for a job as a computer programmer with the Port Authority, but I was a level C and computer programming was a level B and they would not let anybody cross that line. That was in 1967. Maybe they do it now, but they wouldn't give somebody an opportunity to move from that level, which was stupid. I would have felt safer getting a job with their program, but they wouldn't take me so I did a few things.

I went to a place called the Advertiser Club and they had a free job finding forum which was very interesting. They had a very definite technique, a cover letter that draws people's attention to your résumé and if you want to be moving into a new field, you pick something that's going to sell yourself. I wrote that I wanted to be a computer programmer and brought up a very true incident that happened to me when I worked in export as a secretary. I had a job where I worked for the traffic manager and made out export documents. They dealt with several countries and I was really very efficient, which .as a computer programmer is an important feature. If the export documents weren't in good order, they would have to pay fines on the other side. I was very efficient, so that's what I put as my qualifications in a cover letter. And then I used the fact that I was a Spanish major and very good in grammar and languages.

So there I was, going to the Advertising Club and my letter and résumé were far from perfect, but I was trying. What they told you to do was to call up the companies that you would like to work for, .find the correct person to whom you should address the letter. Get their annual report so you begin to know something about the company, and they don't recommend that you go to agencies.

Well, I went to some agencies which I think is the approach most people would do, and one young girl was very honest with me. She said to me point blank, "I can't send you out on this trainee job, because of your age." She was honest with me. That was before they had the laws. The Advertising Club's method would tell you, "You gotta be aware of the fact, but be prepared with your answers, and don't bring age to the forefront which is what a lot of people do."

I went to a life insurance company and they granted me an interview, and at that time you had to take these long computer programming tests. They probably do it for schools now, but at the time, it was a very expensive way to find out your abilities. I was there the whole day, and I had a strong feeling they would reject me because of age. One of the things that they suggested to me at the Advertising Club was that if they offer you a job, take five years off of your age. Then when you get the job, tell them. I did that.

I had to fill out this form in the employment office and I adjusted high school and everything by five years. I added five to every date and I did not sign where they asked, "Is everything you said here true?" So I gave it to the guy and he never saw that I didn't sign it. He sends me to this guy who interviewed me and he had all these big flow charts of what we could do with some theoretical situations, and we talked and he offered me the job. I also put down a very minimum salary, because I was willing to take anything just to get my foot in the door. Then I went back to personnel, and I walk in and he's a very nice young guy.

By then he knew that the job had been offered to me and I closed the door and said, "I have something to tell you. I lied by five years. I'm a very honest person; I think you can realize why I did it." At first he said, "That's against the law." He was really a nice guy; he gave me a whole new application to fill out honestly and I said, "Do you want me to tell the interviewer?" He said, "No that's all right." I'm really a very quiet, shy kind of person and yet, I guess certain things I'll do like that.

I'm now sixty-three and I am going to take early retirement. I've been working at the same company for twenty-two years. As a secretary, I never made it to an executive level because I hated it. The work at my current company is so much more complicated, and I made it to Project Manager. I would never have dreamt that I would have such a responsible job, because of my beginning. I had an older sister and brother who did everything. I was the little one; I never pushed. I'm not aggressive, but somehow I worked my way up. I did it the hard way, and I had one or two managers who were very good for me and they pushed me ahead too. I moved up, and I had a lot of responsibility.

I became a junior programmer, a senior programmer then a project leader. I never had the highest job, but I became very knowledgeable in one of their system's positions. I did programming and some designing. I did specifications that other programmers would carry out. I had to be on call every single month with a beeper when I didn't have a terminal at home. Every month they ran statements and if they had problems like something happens and the computer stops, I'd get a call. I went in at two or three o'clock in the morning sometimes.

The first times I got called in, I used to get terrified, because you're really under pressure. I mean, the whole world is waiting, "Oh my God, what if I can't solve it?" But then I got so good at this, I used to get a big kick out of it and I said if anyone could solve it, I could. I once had some guy come in on New Year's, a real manager type. I had to come in, because he couldn't solve the problem. I used to get a big kick out of that, because no one knew the programs like I did.

About three years ago things changed which I was very hurt about, but it was good that it all happened. At one point, they started to hire people over me, one person, two people. I'm now further away from the guy who I originally reported to. I wouldn't be comfortable with that managerial kind of work anyway and it wasn't so bad, because they still needed me for statements. But then, in computer work, they were going to completely redesign their customer statements and they took me off Customer Statements and I was put on a totally different system. I went from being a chief honcho to being a programmer with the same salary though, and I still have my title.

The field has changed so much in twenty years. Underneath my nose, this thing is changing too rapidly. I could stay there until I'm sixty five, no one's going to push me out and I've gotten over the initial hurt. You know, when you're knocked off your pedestal, it's like, "You don't need me anymore." And that's good in a way, because I was not the one to be in on the redesigning of the system.

There's a whole new technology and they needed someone with fresh eyes to look at it. I did a lot of good stuff for them and when I started, I never ever thought of retiring.

I used the same kind of approach--I went to NYU. They have wonderful courses on retirement, like "After 55, what next?" and, "Can you afford to retire?" I mean it's a similar technique as I used in my past, and I met one woman that I took a course with who is a career counselor and does a lot of work with retired people. I took this course and I thought, maybe I want another career. I mean, what do I do when I retire?

So I went to NYU and in one of these retirement courses you get a whole list of positions you can volunteer in. One of the teacher's theories was, "If there's some kind of work you're thinking of doing, try it as a volunteer." It's a very good way to get into it. So I thought I might be interested, but what could I do at this point? Maybe I'll look into Geriatrics. So I went to the library and read up on Geriatrics.

There were books that describe careers and I read about that and I didn't think I'd be interested. So I'm looking at these different kinds of volunteer jobs and one of them was speaking English with people at "English in Action," which is part of the English Speaking Union. Then I started to hear about teaching English as a second language. I called up this English speaking class and volunteered.

All you do is you go there and you just speak. These people just want to converse in English. So I went there and I had some wonderful experiences. I really liked it. I found it fun, but I found it frustrating because it wasn't enough just to talk to them. I saw that I wanted to teach. I think that was really my calling; I was supposed to be a teacher! When I used to play bridge and I would explain things to people I was playing with, they'd say, "You can explain it really well, you're a good teacher."

I found out that it was a very open field, that they really need people in it and age wasn't a problem; now I have to worry about age even more! I found out you have to have a Master's Degree. I said hmm, let me look into this. So I had what was a very traumatic experience for me.

I graduated from College in 1948, and I went to a fortieth reunion in 1988. It was great. I went for the first time in all those years and I was going to get information about the Master's Program. The way I felt was, I knew nothing about this whole thing and I went in there and I thought they're going to look at me like "What are you some old lady?" I mean I was just terrified that they were going to look at me and say, "What's the matter with you? You want to take a Masters?" I was really nervous.

I went and they treated me like a human being! They couldn't have been nicer about it! They gave me all the information and I had to talk to this doctor who was the head of the department and he was very nice. He told me that he only could take eighty people 'cause they're the least expensive of all the colleges. They do have a big demand and I thought, I'll never get into that. This is wild; he was really a crazy guy. He said "I just got this letter in the mail where they need tutors. They're asking me for tutors for September at the community college," and he gives me the name of the person to call to tutor! Here I was interested in maybe taking the Master's and getting into it and instead of saying, "What are you, some kind of a crazy lady? He tells me that someone's looking for tutors and suggests that I go.

The first term I did it was with no qualifications. I had students from Haiti, a Korean guy, a Chinese fellow, all nice young students. Then I decided that I'm not going to go for a Master's at this point. The New School has recently started a certificate program and I'm now registered. Since I started, all sorts of things have opened up and I know so much more about it. I went to a convention last year. There's a big convention at the Sheraton Hotel, Teaching English As A Second Language. They have one every year because now it's a big field. I feel that I'll be able to get a job doing it and age is really not a barrier.

The older I get, the more I enjoy life. When I was very young, my motivation was just to do well and that's because I was brainwashed and that's horrible. I enjoyed school when I was young, but I didn't really enjoy what I was doing; it was just how well did I do it! There was a lot of competitiveness. My attitude is changing a great deal just because of age--hitting like sixty.

I had an older brother; we had a close relationship in a sense. It was a love/hate relationship; I realize it now. I guess I was jealous of him, because he was a boy. He was definitely more important, no matter what anyone said and he was very smart. The truth is I thought I was dumb, because my sister and brother were such good students. I thought I couldn't do what they did and I went to school with, "Oh you're Jeans sister". Everywhere I went, that's what I was. I had no sense of identity.

I love my family; I don't like them. One of the things that meant a lot to me and that gave me tremendous confidence was that I was successful in a career. That meant so much to me, that I was successful in a career that I have a lot of respect for. I'm not a screaming success. There are people who worked for me who went over and beyond what I did, but from where I came, I had a successful career.

I hope I will enjoy becoming a teacher. There are times I feel confident and there are times I'm anxious, but it is different when you're thinking about a career and you don't have to rely on it for your entire income. When I was forty, I knew I had many years to work. I had no one to fall back on. When I took the job as a programmer, I left a very secure semi-civil-service job and I threw myself into private industry. A year after I got into programming, they had a terrible crash on Wall Street. I survived it. They let twenty per cent of the company go.

I didn't used to know what made me tick. I really know a lot about myself now. I know my good points and I know my shortcomings. I've had years of therapy and I wouldn't trade that experience for anything. Therapy for me was always labeled supportive therapy. It seems that I needed support. There were no great personality changes; that's not what I needed. I just needed support for confidence.

When I first went to a psychiatrist, I was living with my mother and I didn't tell her why I was coming home late. This went on week after week. I'll never forget this one night she said to me, "Don't you think it's about time I know where you go?" She probably thought, and she should have been very happy, that I was having an affair with someone. Little did she know men didn't get that close to me. I said to her, "You really want to know where I'm going? I'm going to a psychiatrist," and you know what her answer was? "If you needed a psychiatrist, I would have taken you." But she and I didn't have a good relationship. When I got into therapy, our relationship improved, because I wasn't looking for her anymore and I understood her and that was a first step for me.

I'm confident that it's all going to work out. At first when I used to think about telling my boss that I was resigning, I thought I was going to cry. Now, I feel totally different, I feel very excited about it. It is going to be an adjustment, but I'm getting used to it.

Into It

Amos
Nature Photographer

I've tried in one way to disappear by going to other places of the world. And one place that I went to very often in my childhood was into books, books which described the great explorers like Degamon, Magellan, Captain Cook, and Marco Polo. Those people fascinated me. But what was fascinating more than anything was not just the names, it was the sea voyages that they took. The trauma and the trials and the experience and the success that they had throughout a long period of time.

The history of photojournalism almost demands that the photographer be committed to exploring life as well as a dedication to taking pictures. It is a challenge few are willing to take and fewer able to succeed.

I'm here 15 years and I came to the States not knowing what I'm looking for. I didn't have anything in particular in mind, except that I wanted to study. I always wanted to study film and television and on the periphery, the desire to fulfill my bigger dream to explore the world. Before I came here, I traveled for almost two years. I traveled throughout the world with a backpack and a few friends and we went throughout Southeast Asia and South America until we came here. We did everything, traveled on the back of a camel, a horse, by bus, or by foot. We smuggled things across borders. We smuggled boats for people from one part of the world to another and sold goods on the black market. Sometimes we smuggled weapons. All over Southeast Asia it's a very big business: Hong Kong, China, Pakistan, Afghanistan, India, also Mongolia and Manchuria and eventually I came here.

I knew what I wanted, but I was not determined about it. There was not really something that burned inside me-- "That is what I want to do!" I was here for about two years, but I was illegal, so it was very difficult to do different things, or even to go to school. And money, of course, was always a problem. There were a lot of complications with my becoming legal in this country. It was really a very trying period of time because on the one hand, every day I looked out and I could see the Statue of Liberty but inside I did not feel free to do what I wanted to do. I was limited. As soon as I got the green card I decided, no matter what, I'm going to do it and I opened a business.

At first, I was converting lofts, commercial spaces to residential. Then I started organizing scuba diving trips taking people to different places around the world and I thought that it would give me the chance to really do the exploration that I wanted to do. I felt that I was bringing something new to the American public, because the knowledge of the world at the time was very limited here for the average person. I had the information because I was there and I was able to set up, to create logistics that most Americans never dared--to go from New York or New Jersey to the Indian Ocean and into the South Pacific or to the Red Sea.

I thought if I do that as a business, it also would give me the chance to photograph at the same time, which was always my desire. Now I could take the camera and put it under water. In Israel I did not have the chance to do that because of the public stigma, public opinion and also my parents were saying "It is not a job. You are not a doctor, you are not a lawyer, you're not a builder and you're not a soldier. What the hell are you going into Liberal Arts for? Are you crazy? Besides doing Liberal Arts, traveling around the world! How then can you speak any other languages, like English or Italian or French?" I did not speak any of those languages. It was not encouraged in me and being a photographer in Israel was not encouraged either.

My father used to call me a prostitute because I was going to do photography. I used to work as a photographer's assistant for a fashion photographer in Israel. And I would work on the weekend which is the Sabbath in Israel and most places are closed, so you can do certain things that during the week you can't, because they are full of people. I had a very tough relationship with my father. Practically speaking, he abused me physically, not by molesting, but by beating me continuously, because of whatever anger that was in him or disappointment with life.

Almost anything I wanted to do or anything I thought about was very difficult, almost impossible. At school I had a very difficult time to express myself because they called me a maverick or they thought that I'm out of my mind. I was always thinking about those kinds of things that never could happen and eventually they have happened. I was talking about either electronics or social problems or social issues, the changes of the human race. I wrote compositions and the teachers would call my parents and say, "What does this kid read?!" I was reading a lot of newspapers at the time and again, back into the books, and my mind was what's happening. In history and science you have a chance to go, to discover for the future. So I would go into space travel. They could not understand where I was coming from. It was nothing they were teaching at the time.

Jacques Cousteau started to create some changes in the world of diving, and Jules Vern with his books, and the American Nuclear Submarine Program. All those things started to really become part of my imagination and I could see myself doing those things. So I found photography and exploration. I found the expression of them in underwater, either traveling to some places or going under water and continuing to explore with a camera. I was not yet a professional.

I contracted with a local dive shop and at first their thinking was very narrow-minded. They could not see the world as a global place, an arena to play in. For them it was only to go from here to New Jersey, or from here to the Caribbean. So I said, what big thing?! You're taking the same plane, and you fly another ten hours. It's the same thing. It's the flight; that's all it is. You don't have to even shake your hands to do that. So I had to go on my own to do that. I had to drive a cab during the night, and during the day I did the business. I placed small ads in a magazine and people answered back. I started with the specialty magazine that was dealing with this sport. In this case, it was a skin diving magazine. I placed a small ad there and that's how it started.

The first trip was with four people. Naturally, I took them to the place which I knew best at the time, which was the Red Sea and the Sinai Desert when Israel was still in control of the Sinai. And then on the second trip, I took only another four people. I did not make money, of course in the beginning, but it was just to create the momentum. After the second time that I was there, I realized that there is a bigger potential. I saw a boat that was sitting in Israel and doing almost nothing and I said, there's a better idea. Rather take Americans, who don't like to be roughing it out in the desert or sitting on the camels, put them on a boat, give them an air conditioned room and enough fresh water and put in diving all the time and they will be very happy. And sure enough in 1978, I was on a live-on-board dive boat on the Red Sea. And we had the compressor, the tanks, everything aboard the boat, and from there we go diving.

165

We traveled on the ocean for ten days and went diving in one of the most spectacular reefs in the world, and diving all day long so people got a chance to go more than one or two times a day. Then I started taking my camera under water. I had the money to buy this camera, the Nikonos, which is a special camera made by Nikon, to go under water. And then I had to buy a housing to fit my camera. So that's what took time, because it took money to do that. And the boat is practically a floating, diving resort.

I put a portable photo lab on board and we could develop slides on the boat from the shooting during the day. I was developing for everybody. People shoot during the day and in the evenings I would develop the rolls and do all the chemicals and changes. There was a crew on the boat, but I did most of the dive mastering, meaning the tour guiding of the people under water, teaching them underwater photography. For me it was schooling, and that is when I started my schooling as well. So I realized then that rather than go to school, I can benefit from that experience. I was traveling a lot between the United States and Israel, United States and Ecuador, all over the world and leading groups.

I realized how I should teach myself and other people at the same time. I developed a program in which I hired one of the world's experts to lead and to be the guest lecturer on board the trip. And we had only about ten or twelve people. I hired either a photographer or a marine biologist or cinematographer to be a guest lecturer on board and at the same time, I will have a chance to learn. Those experts will have probably one of the first chances they had to get out of the country, because otherwise, how do they get to those remote places?

It started in 1979 with David Doubilet, the photographer of National Geographic. For two weeks, we were living in the same quarters. And then with Stan Waterman. Stan is a cinematographer. In marine biology, we worked with Doctor Eugene Clark and Doctor Sylvia Earn. She is today the chief scientist of NOAA (National Oceanic Atmospheric Administration.) That's how I continued to explore my own work and get my own understanding of the marine world and also have the chance to see how the pro works and from them, develop my own style.

I did not think about how to pay them at the time. Sometimes, I guess when you don't know, it's better than when you know. The only thing I had was my own burning desire. That's it; nothing else could come into my thinking. So I never weighed this against that. I just came to them and said that's what I want. And I'm willing to pay x amount of money. They were very happy. They were out of their seats when I offered, because they never got an offer like that before--work and get paid! And here is a doctor, or a dean of a university or a member of the faculty and here she got a free trip! Up until now, she was scratching out of the wall to get some dollars to go on a trip and now somebody gave it to her for free.

Now it's a monster in the industry, because anyone of those leaders are asking for a lot of money and it has become very complicated and some of those people are doing their own trips today. Those who used to be a guest lecturer today, like Doctor Gini Clark, for example, is running her own trips. She negotiates with boats.

We made a living out of that and after awhile, I realized that I did not have a chance to explore anymore my own photography. There came a point of a clash between the photography and the business. The artist in me started to come out more and more, rather than the business person and also the business started to take a really heavy pounding because of the terrorist activity. 1986 and 1987 is when hostages were starting to be taken and with the TWA kidnapping there was a lot of damage happening to our business which was in a lot of third world countries. We were invested heavily, so I decided to close the business. It did not make sense to me anymore to continue that unless I wanted to devote all of my attention to it. I left with a treasure of underwater pictures. So I thought, what do I do with that now?

There were two pivotal years during which I did not yet trust the artist in myself. However, I did not have anything else better to do, except driving a cab or finding some other kind of odd jobs. I went with the pictures around the city to some of the stock photography houses. That's all I had in my hand. Everybody was stunned when they saw the pictures. They said, "Where have you stored them, where did you keep them?" They were looking for this kind of material. So that's how I started and I've signed a contract with one agency, one of the largest stock photography organizations in the world.

I continued to find events and places around the world which I was interested in and I went there and photographed. And then I realized that for my professional development, something has to happen so I started teaching and Nikon, through the Nikonos

Underwater Division had a program which was taken from my original program in the early eighties to send professional photographers on location to the Caribbean to teach how to take a picture under water. Also, I still lead scuba diving expeditions to different parts of the world, about six or eight of them during the year, which will give me the opportunity also to be in different parts of the world and continue to photograph.

The only formal training I'm doing now is short courses in aspects, in which I don't feel that I'm solid enough. I may know it intuitively, but I don't know it geometrically and mathematically like lighting in different conditions, multiple strobes and all kinds of new techniques with new lenses, and what they do to light and how they can be compatible with working under water.

The Photo Expo, which is once a year, has a big convention in The Javits Center so photographers and photo agencies and camera makers from all over the world can come and show their goods, and they have seminars. I go for three or four days and I see how I can adapt equipment from land photography and take it under water. I work a lot on the concept of adaptation of materials and I go to some optician or technician and I work with them. I tell them what my problem is, and they try to help me to solve it. I contact the manufacturer and I call the engineering department and tell them about a problem with a lens and how the lens reacts underwater. So this engineer goes back to his drawing board and does all the computations, or he calls somebody else and eventually they give me the information. And they like it, because for them it is different than what they do everyday; they like these kinds of challenges.

That's what entices me; I only live for challenges, only for experiences, to go onto something new. Personally, I don't have time to sit in a library, not that I don't have time; I will not make the time. I'm not a library type. I fall asleep if I sit there and search. There are people who do it for fun and they enjoy doing it, so give them the fun and in return, give it to me and together we all benefit. And then, if I do something nice, I send them a picture or two and they are very pleased, so it is not an exchange of dollars only, but personal satisfaction.

You can make a good living out of this, but you have to be very focused and very determined about what you want to do. It does not happen easily and there is competition. More and more people do this today and technology is moving very rapidly. You have to be on the edge of that, so you have to take your money and invest all the time in research and development. You have to do a lot of trial and error; you do a lot of personal assignments which means that you have to be self-motivated.

Nobody will assign you anything unless you show that you can really do the work. There are only about two photographers in the world who do underwater pictures for National Geographic. However, there are about ten very prolific and leading underwater photographers. In addition to that, there are thousands of people who use cameras under water. And that's the reason why I started to break away from only underwater and am expanding to do some other, what they call, "risk photography" or "adventure/travel" photography. "Free Jumping", mountain climbing, kayaking are those kinds of sports that can be documented to freeze the moment of life that passes by and never returns again.

I think the potential in anything to do with the environment for the next decade, will continue on an even pace compared to high-tech, or fashion or compared to corporate photography. It will have a tremendous effect on the business. There will be a continued interest in the environment in this decade so whatever picture there is of a human being involved with the environment, no matter in what aspect will be something that is in demand.

Today, there are several schools which specialize in underwater photography. One of them is Brooks Institute in Santa Barbara, California which is very well known for their curriculum in photography in general and they also teach underwater photography. And they are terrific! They are great to do adventure/travel. I know there are many seminars around the country which are taught by photographers. These are one week courses which have a leading photographer come in who gives a lecture or teaches.

My belief is you can go to The School of Visual Arts in New York, or you can go to The Institute of Photography, and there are many schools of photography around the country, but it is mostly technical. I don't know, since I have not been to any of them, if they really encourage your personal style and encourage your artistic value. They may teach you what the artistic trend of today is, because that's what they know, but they don't know about what will be in the future.

The individual student must be willing to put themselves on the line and create their own work and be proud of it. School does not teach you that. School teaches you the technology and the techniques which you have to know. But techniques I can learn from a book, and just buy the camera and go out and shoot and learn from experience. That's what you feel, because it is art. I'm a creator. The artist needs to believe in himself or herself and have great self-esteem and confidence and to some extent, maybe be a little eccentric to believe and be willing to live in a medium.

Most photographers are very much into talking about their work and giving ideas or advice to start in photography. Go and ask the expert, the people who already do something. That's one way to start in a business. I always ask the question when I meet somebody in the business, "Can you recommend somebody I can talk to?" And I learn from them.

You have a guide for representatives, you have a guide for stock house photographers, a directory for all the companies in America who use advertising. I have books here I've never looked at. I like the personal contact. It's a very good thing to look at everything, however either way, it demands some money. You need to send them something to introduce yourself, so you have to produce this elaborate piece of introduction, the portfolio and you don't just send a portfolio to somebody. That's a very expensive thing, just processing your images is expensive. You send them an introductory card, like a business card but much larger, together with a picture and an illustration. Send it in the mail with something in your handwriting like, "If you want to see more, please call..." Or, "If you like them, I have more of the same or different ones," something that will entice. You do it several times throughout the year until eventually, those buyers of art work will eventually need work and they will call you, "Oh, I remember you." So your card has to be special and unique so they remember, because they're getting a lot of them everyday from everyone who is starting a business. You have to do that and then pick up the phone and call and if they ask you for the work, you have to be able to send more out to them.

I know many people who unfortunately get stuck in being a photographer's assistant. What happens when you become an assistant is that you become more of a technical worker to this photographer. Very rarely does the photographer really involve his or her assistant in the day-by-day decisions, like lighting and what they see in their minds, and what eventually they get on the film. They don't do that. I don't think they have the time for that. It is the responsibility of the assistant to hold the umbrella and the light, make sure that there is fuel in the tank, and a passport, and enough money and you're not really able to think artistically. I recommend it providing you get enough confidence that after a year or two, which ever amount of years you want to learn about all different forms of photography, that you stop, take the risk and go on your own. It is risk. It is really entrepreneurial with a capital E.

I do not have a family, because if I did I know that I could not have the style of life that I have. The women that have been in my life do not think that this would be the most desirable situation for them, to be married to somebody like me and all the time I'm going away to different places. If that's what you want in life, to have a family and career, then you probably can achieve that too. There is nothing that you want that you cannot achieve. It is a question of what you are willing to give up for that. The other question is what your spouse is willing to give up for that.

I prefer the artist, it is more natural. I don't have to think about it twice. I don't have to try to balance so many things at the same time or other peoples wishes, desires and wants, and law and order or anything else. When you're out, when you are an artist, you forget about law and order; they do not exist. If they exist, you are not an artist anymore, or maybe you are, but a different kind of artist. When I create, everything is possible. It does not mean always the sun is rising on the left corner of the picture. It can't, because that is a boring picture. Not always is the subject the center in a picture! You have to move things around. You have to see. Create something that people did not see up until now. Create an angle that people are not used to look at. You cannot look at the world always from whatever is the average height of people in America. Stop it, because then everything looks the same.

For me it is very engrossing and I get very involved in what I do. I don't think of a camera as a tool. A camera is only an extension of my eye and looking through the camera, it becomes almost one with my hands. For me, it is important to be involved in what I do, whether it is on a boat, on the back of a horse, under water, while I'm flying or while I'm jumping from a plane or whatever. Then I can create the best images. I don't think about the law. Only the law of gravity will apply to me. That's the only law which is important. I always need to fall in a way in which I will be able to stand up.

If you want to be a football player and if you want to be a writer or a physicist, whatever you want most to try, go out and try it. Let

him go through an experience and really get engrossed forever, or
throw it out of the window. Because a person at twelve or fourteen
or even at twenty, I don't think is yet mature enough to make a
decision about what they want to do for their life or for part of their
life. They don't know and I think it is a mistake, the pressure that
society puts on people. What I would like to encourage is, remember
and pursue what you really like. If you want to be a football player,
try to go to a football team and really be on a team and see how you
get along with the other men and how you really get punched and feel
successful in that. And if you want to be a physicist, let's see you take
extra classes. Let's see you do the extra work that is necessary to be
one of the best. The same thing is true in photography.

My job seems to be very glorious or very spectacular to some
people. Let me see you take your own camera, wake up at four
o'clock in the morning, stand on top of a building or on the Hudson
River and take a picture with the sun rising over the river and
something really different. Do it more than one morning. Do it 365
days a year until eventually, you're able to capture a picture which
nobody ever before was able to catch. Then when editors see that
you have determination, you have a drive, you will be the person they
want. Because when I send you to the Persian Gulf for the war, I
know you are going to bring me a picture that nobody else will.
That's what it takes. It takes the extra step, not just the desire. It is in
your mind, so act on your own desire.

If you cannot buy a camera, I understand. Somebody is probably
willing to loan you a camera or to somehow get a camera for you.
But eventually, you have to be the one to do it, to stay when it's
stormy outside and when it's snowing in order to take the special
picture. Or go out into the countryside when there is lightning and
take a picture of the sky. Those are the ones that make the
difference. It is not the picture of a wedding or a picture of the party
of the family at home that you can use to show how good you are.

I'm now doing more than underwater photography and I'm
getting involved in other aspects like looking at adventure, travel,
above water and in the air. And getting involved also in leading
different organizations and groups into doing something of this
nature. I'm also getting more involved now in the movie world of
photography, working as second camera man. At least I will have the
knowledge and I will be able to apply myself on different levels. I like
the aesthetic of movement and also the outdoors. Adventure travel is

not yet as competitive, so it is giving me some kind of advantage. Naturally, it is an evolving situation. It is a place where I'll be able to really learn from the mistakes I made before, not to repeat being just focused on one business. Now I have the chance to go into something a little bit different, between being a lecturer and leading expeditions.

People today ask a lot of questions about job skills. We forget about the uniqueness of the individual. I think that is a key, more than learning from Van Gogh and how he did it and what kind of person he was, or Mozart or Beethoven or any one of those. There is no way that I'm going to copy Francis Coppola or Steven Spielberg, who is one of my heroes in photography, or Ansel Adams--I'm not Ansel Adams. However, there is something else in me or something else in other superb underwater photographers. They act on their internal calling, on their own inspiration, on their own intuition. They really act on it, and that's what makes them great. So no matter what you want, if you really feel so good about it, you take action on it and you will be what you want to be.

You can have all the money in the world, you can have all the connections, but you are not going to be who you want to be, unless you act on it, no matter what. You're not going to make this note of music unless you get out of bed in the middle of the night, and you put on the bow the note of music that comes into your head.

What happens in someone's life when either they don't listen to themselves or they do? From the moment that they start listening to themselves and then recognize what is happening to them, what is the brain or the heart or the intuition saying? It is not important how strong or how weak you are, or what is the color of my eyes or color of my hair and what is my education and what is my upbringing, how many scholarships I have. None of this makes any difference. It is not a question about what kind of a person I am; the question is what does it takes to move a person to listen?

Into It

Susan
Animal Social Worker

I'm a social worker in the world's largest animal hospital. It's a very high tech place. We do many of the things that go on in human hospitals. I see one half of the pets. I see the people who have a good deal of attachment to their pets, and mostly they're like family. I see the staff and I talk to people whose family member is seriously ill or injured or has died and they have tough decisions to make, or they have tough things to experience and they need somebody to talk to.

We try to pick doctors who are compassionate, kind and who care about human beings, as well. So they obviously do most of it. I get the cases where somebody's really stuck or needs a lot more time than the veterinary can give--or needs maybe, a neutral person.

Sometimes because of people's experiences, they're a little suspicious. Their grandmother was badly treated in the human hospital, so they're a little suspicious about doctors in general. The doctors are saying, "Your dog really needs surgery," and they're just not so sure. "How do I know they're not just trying to make money off my pet? How do I know they're not doing some research experiment and they want to use my pet as a guinea pig? She's such a nice young woman, I don't want to hurt her feelings, but I just don't want to go that far, and I don't know how to tell her that--she's the doctor."

They need somebody who has no stake in the medicine, who they know is safe to talk to. They know that whatever they say is confidential--they're not going to run back and tell anybody else. I'm not going to mistreat their loved one because of something they said. I'm safe.

I was trained as a social worker, not a veterinarian although I wanted to be a veterinarian at one point when I was a kid. But it's that relationship that intrigues me. It's why I went back to school--to look at that connection, the place where they cross over. I think everybody that's involved in the human-animal bond field got there the same way. It was because you had some sort of experience as a kid. You said, wow, this is important or this is needed. This makes me feel good, or I bet it would make other people feel good--that draws you to this.

People who choose to focus on animals really focus on animals, and since they are not particularly interested in people, do have a different headset. I've always loved animals and I've always been interested in them, curious about them, got a lot of pleasure out of being with them and I know that if you had told me when I was 8 or 18 that there would be a job like this, I could have told you then that I would want it. But of course, it didn't exist then. The field didn't exist and the awareness really didn't exist then.

At a certain point after I had some life experience, I realized I was very interested and concerned about certain kinds of problems that involved people. I liked both one on one relationships or helping some group of people who have had a problem fix that problem. I also liked teaching them the ropes so that they knew how to play the game and so they wouldn't need me to intercede for them. And I also liked that larger picture--what are the big issues. How were different people trying to approach this problem and I knew I was going to have to go back to school. I said ok, what's the name of that job that lets you do that stuff? And that turned out to be Social Work. Because I'm very clearly the kind of person who gets involved with people, learns about a problem, and says well, I'm going to personally do something about it, Social Work seemed to be the right route for me to do that.

I became a social worker because of the kind of person I am. I don't ask people questions or show interest in them, because I'm a Social Worker; it went the other way. And there's still a big part of me that says, I can't believe I get paid to do this. You mean there's a job where you get to do this? And they pay you too? But the discipline, the training is so much a part of me now, that it's very hard for me to separate it.

A case that I had today was a pet that had been hit by a car--a young, healthy, wonderful pet who had a spinal cord injury so that, as the doctor said, from here up it's fine but from here down it's dead. Unlike human paraplegics, the dog lives more in his body, is more confined to his body and his being. I used to work with human paraplegics. They can play cards, they can go to college, they can watch television, they can hang out with their friends. They can get on a bus that has a wheelchair lift, they can make love, they can eat wonderful food, they have a great richness to their life--many ways to distract themselves from what's happened to them. A dog doesn't, so you can make some accommodations for the dog but the dog is maybe...I want to say, is not going to be happy, but given whatever way we have of assessing a dog's comfort with the ability to function, it is harder to make it ok for them than it is to make it ok for the person.

So the pet was euthanized and it was very painful for the family, and very painful for the doctor. I guess we think of it as helping someone to die who's dying already. The question mostly, not always, but mostly isn't--is this dog, cat, bird going to die anyway? The question is how is this pet going to die? Is this pet going to die hard or easy? Is the family going to be present or not? And that's how the people that I deal with, want to approach it, because for them, it's family. I think 85 percent of how I am is just taking people seriously. So if it were you, I would help you tell your story and I would try to find out what happened, what was going on for you and what it seemed like for you.

I've loved animals as long as I can remember. I had my first pet when I was 4, a dog. Got my next pet at 6 which was a parrot. I was very interested in science as a child, went through a period of wanting to be a veterinarian, realized I was squeamish, realized I could get past being squeamish, but by that time had figured out that I couldn't add. My math was terrible. That was going to make hard science tough. In college I majored in English and almost had a double major in anthropology.

I took a career evaluation test at a time when people didn't do this. She had to give me the male test, because that's where the good jobs were--there were male tests, there were female tests. And my top 5 jobs, my A category jobs were: physician, musician, psychiatrist, psychologist, minister and I said, boy this was so unhelpful--this doesn't tell me a thing. This doesn't help. So I forgot all about it and I went on and majored in English and anthropology, worked, got married, had children, worked. When I was pregnant with my second child, I said, ok I have to go back to school. What is it that I've liked and what haven't I liked and what do I want to do more of? I liked helping people, solving problems. I liked sitting down and hearing your story and helping you get to the real heart of your soul, which was really the point here.

I'm not very brave about walking up to people and saying "Hi!" But I knew that it wasn't going to work to sit in my office, and I was real curious. So that's what I did. I hung out in the night pharmacy and read stuff and asked questions and said, "Could I watch you do this case?" And I always felt, and I guess I have been told, that part of my job was to sensitize--that's the doctors word.

I felt that part of my job was to teach them, to reinforce the good things they were doing. If I watched a doctor do really well with a case and I said, gee if I were a client, what she just said would really make me feel good. What he just did made me feel like I was in good hands. So I would go up to these doctors afterwards and I'd say, "Hey Bob, remember that case from yesterday?" And Bob would always back up, "Yea..." And I'd say, "Remember when you kept your hands on the dog while you were explaining that he had cancer?" "Yea..." They looked like they were going to get hit. I'd say "That was really great the way you did that. It made them feel much better." "Yea?!" "Bob, that's the whole thing. I just want to tell you what a great job you did." And they'd unwind and say, "Gee, thanks." So I began to realize that there was a lot of stress there for a lot of reasons, and that mostly what they heard about were the mistakes and not the good things and certainly no one was paying a whole lot of attention to the client relations.

So from the beginning, in addition to working with the clients, I work with the staff teaching them but also supporting them, trying to be there for them. I'm learning from them. They were teaching me a lot and they were so open.

There aren't a lot of people who do what I do in an institutional setting. There are a lot of reasons for that. It's been nine and a half years that I've been here and it's still a handful. So I asked myself, why did it work here, 'cause it really did work here. It worked, and it worked fast. It didn't take five years of working it through with various departments to see who would get to own it and fight it out. Once the director could feel that it was time to do it, he could pull it off right away. I think it was a good match--me and this place.

When you start something new, you have to have some sense of what you think you're going to do, and you have to tell the people when you get there or before you get there, what it is you're proposing to do. But since it was a totally brand new concept, there's no way that they could really know what they're going to do. You have to tell them something first, but there's no way that they could get it. So then you have to go there and live it out for them and make yourself useful, and be in a room when they come in.

About three or four months after I had gotten there, one of the people from medical records came up to me and she said "You know, it's really odd. It almost seems as though we sent a letter to all of our clients saying that we have a social worker here now, because since you got here, I never saw so many sad people in my life." I hope what she was trying to say was, "I never noticed there were so many sad people." Once you can do something about a problem, you can afford to notice it.

I am a catalyst. That's why I don't have to do it all. The fact that there is a social worker here makes it ok to think about it and it's ok to feel this way. Many more of my cards are given out than ever result in clients at my door, but they carry that card around and they feel better because the fact that there is a social staff means that it's ok to feel that way. And the doctors don't always have to call me because they tell me they can afford to listen to their clients talk about that fact--that their husband just left them and they just got laid off from work. Because now they know if it gets out of hand, there's somebody they can call. I think some of the value of this is symbolic, catalytic.

In one of my classes, my doctoral class, we read a book called "Educating The Reflective Practitioner" and they talk about that discovery experience within ourselves. What is that? Is that just some airy thing that you can't pin down and doesn't mean anything? And what leads to that sudden ability to handle something that's a little different from anything you ever had before. It is partly the preparation. It doesn't happen in a vacuum and you don't always see it. You see it when you're ready to see it. You see what you believe. You'd have to have some sense, not just that it could happen to you or for you, but that it could happen at all--there's space for it in the universe.

If you're a child of poverty, generation after generation of poverty, and nobody you know went to college, you wouldn't necessarily realize that you could go to college, but you might get there. It would be very hard to invent the idea of college if it didn't exist in the universe. That's harder.

I went to a wonderful school and I noticed that my friends from school had some belief expectation sense that you're allowed to pursue your interests and put together your own thing. None of the people that I'm really close to from college are doing jobs that existed when we got out. I think somehow what got nurtured in us was that you have to have enough determination and strength to say, "Even though you're all telling me that this isn't ok, I think it's ok and I'm going to do it anyway."

In our culture, grieving is a part of the death you care a lot about. Everybody's different. There is no right way to grieve or deal with death. Stuff that maybe would get you sent to Bellevue, like you hear things that aren't there, you see things that aren't there, sudden emotional outbursts, or you get totally numb and nonresponsive. That sounds like you're experiencing some serious emotional decline except that it's normal when you're grieving. Not everybody experiences death in the same way. Some people are more frightened of it than others. I've asked people sometimes when they talk about death or euthanasia, and I can see that they're really having a bad time about asking what that's about.

I have pretty much worked for love. I have gone to school for love; I clearly believe in being happy in general, and that's a decision. I don't think I'm the victim of fate. I don't think that anybody else planned my life out. I don't think that there is a being or karma or anything else that's planned my life or anybody else's. I personally believe you make your own lessons. Life doesn't plan lessons for you.

I never had a career before social work. I had jobs. Within the field of social work, this is my second major field to work in. Part of the reason I went back to school to get my Doctorate was because this interest was clearly not going to blow out anytime soon. The field was going to keep growing, I was still committed to it deeply, still thought there was a lot to learn and a lot to give so it was worth it to go back to school and pursue it in a different way than I had been pursuing it. I still really care deeply about it. I have not gotten tired of the issues. There's still a lot I want to know. But it's not just confined to human-animal interaction. I care about doctors and patients. I care about health policy. I care about jobs, skills. I care about the kinds of transitions in peoples lives.

When I was at my last job, I read a book called "Tactics In The Job Market," and I leafed through it cause it had great exercises to do. I could use this with the students I was counseling. And I was

reading it on the subway--a moment of truth--ah ha! One of the
questions he asks is, "What are two or three job duties that you would
enjoy so much you would practically pay somebody to let you do
them?" Instantly, in my head was--talking to people, and animals.
Wow! Where did that come from? But when it comes that fast, you
have to pay attention to it.

So for arguments sake and so I'll better know how to use this
book, what are all the things I can think of where you talk to people
and you help them to figure things out? Be a veterinarian? Well it's a
little late for that. I don't really want to go back and try to learn math
and biology. Ok--work in a pet store? Oh God, I don't want to sell
dog nail polish. Ok, forget that. Be a tour guide at the zoo? Well,
that could be fun, but I'll bet you don't get paid much to do that and
I'll bet you have to clean cages for about ten years before you work
up to those jobs. Wow--remember that idea you used to have about
how people treat pet loss? Ok, I can put that down.

It was right after that, that I stumbled on that brochure about the
hospital. So when I ask myself now, what are two or three job duties
that I enjoy so much I'd practically pay somebody to let me do them?
It's talking to people and teaching and research, for want of a better
word--the opportunity, ability to investigate things that I'm curious
about, which I've always done, but to do it in a little more systematic
way, so that I can present it to somebody who doesn't automatically
understand their own process.

You get involved in this whole human/animal interaction field
because you love animals--you've had a wonderful experience
somewhere in your life. Maybe you think they are infinitely better
than any person you've ever met in your whole life, so you figure
they're good for people. People should really have this wonderful
experience and you could do great things for them. You get awfully
carried away by your own enthusiasm so you need something, some
mechanism, some approach, to guard you against saying, I totally
believe it! They look happy to me, so let's do more of it.

There are a few steps missing. You may be absolutely right, but
you haven't really established it, and you haven't really given any
consideration to the fact that you're bubbling all over and of course
they're glad to see you because you're bubbling all over and maybe the
dog is happy to do it. Or maybe the dog has something to do with
this person over here quietly being catatonic out of fear.

You have to pay attention to yourself and pay attention to what you like, what makes you feel good, what feels serious and important to you, what feels worth doing, and you have to ask yourself at least once a year, "How do I feel? What am I really enjoying these days? What really feels good? What do I want to do now?" And then you pursue that. You have an absolute right to be happy in your work and you will, according to the research, live longer if you're happy in your work. And you have a right to pursue what you really care about.

When I worked with disabled college students, I would always talk with them first, and somehow we found a short little questionnaire that they could take, that we could plot out on a graph. So before I gave them the questionnaire, I would say, "Tell me what you really like. Tell me what really makes you happy. What are you really good at?" And they would tell me two things, and those two things would always turn up on that test.

But there would always be one that they didn't mention. And I'd say, gee, since your real interest or real ability is in art, tell me about that. "Well, I arrange flowers and I actually have won a lot of awards." Well, what about that? "Oh, you can't do that for a living! That's just what I do 'cause I really love it." So I would say to somebody, pay attention to what you really like and pursue what you really like or what makes you feel really competent or seems important to you. How far wrong can you go?

The worst that'll happen is that you'll have a great hobby and make some friends and in the best of all possible worlds, you'll make a living at it. And if your particular combination of interests and abilities doesn't fit any job title that you know of, then think about creating one.

Where They Are Today

Film/Video Producer
Retired network TV producer, built and rents vacation cabin.

Rehab Councilor for Homeless
Unknown

Child Life Counselor
Unknown

NYC Police Sergeant
Retired, children grown, living in Florida.

Modern Ballet Dancer
Choreographer and dance teacher in NYC.

Musician/Producer
Independent producer, and computer service.

Politician, Town Supervisor
Town Supervisor.

Music Instrument Repair/Performer
Instrument repairman and performer.

Accountant/Olympic Athlete
Finance and athletic administration.

Jeweler/Trucker
Unknown.

Flight Instructor
Career Corporate Pilot.

Human Rights Activist
Administrator, Women's Rights Advocate.

Economist, Low Income Housing
Owner, sailboat customized hardware.

ESL Teacher
Diseased.

Nature Photographer
Internationally known nature photographer.

Animal Social Worker
Consultant, lecturer on pet and animal care.

Into It

Alan
Editor of Into It

My dad loved to use the word "communication" but he was not a particularly good communicator. The only words of advice I ever got from him on how to approach finding a job or career were, "Son, you can be anything you want to be, just don't become a musician." That's what my dad was, and he was very good at what he did, but like many musicians, he got paid only when he worked. This aspect of being self-employed might be a challenge to some, but it's intimidating to others, as it was to my dad. Like the expression goes, "There's no perfect job," and his wasn't.

By profession, I am a clinical engineer with many years of experience overseeing the application of medical technology in New York City hospitals. By desire, I am a photographer with many more years experience than working in my profession. I am an amateur in the classic sense; I photograph what I care about, and I don't make money at it.

I am also an amateur snoopy person who likes to explore and find out how things work. I began this "career" at about age 5. While living in the extreme South-East corner of Yonkers, NY – early fifties – I would take my little red wagon and scour the neighborhood for interesting things people threw in their garbage. Electrical and mechanical things were my specialty; old radios, car parts, clocks, etc. I would drag them home and take them apart to see what was inside. I later did this (without a red wagon) to make a living.

I was born in New York City (Doctor's Hospital, now a luxury condominium), and have lived and worked in and around NYC all my life.

Into It

Other Books by Alan Pakaln

La Festa di San Gennaro

Italian translation of
The Feast of San Gennaro, Little Italy, New York, 1971

New York Shadow:
Behind The Scenes

Eight series
1965 through 2018
New York City
Color and B&W
Coated paper
Quality printing

NYC: B&W
Photographs, 1965-2018

Photographs from
New York Shadow
All B&W
Uncoated paper
Standard printing
Priced accordingly

Robot Desires:
The Social Behavior
of Technology

Also published as:
Invention Is The Mother
of Necessity

Technology itself is driving
the direction of our
inventions. Literally.
And will drive some of us
toward new communities.

The Feast of San Gennaro,
Little Italy, New York, 1971
The People, Food, Activities

B&W portraits, uncoated
paper, standard printing.

Into It

www.ingramcontent.com/pod-product-compliance
Lightning Source LLC
Chambersburg PA
CBHW070117260726
48658CB00001B/136